THE BUDDHA SPEAKS

THE
BUDDHA
SPEAKS

Compiled and edited by Anne Bancroft

SHAMBHALA • *Boston* • 2010

Shambhala Publications, Inc.
Horticultural Hall
300 Massachusetts Avenue
Boston, MA 02115
www.shambhala.com

9 8 7 6 5 4 3 2 1

First Paperback Edition
Printed in the United States of America
♾ This edition is printed on acid-free paper that meets the
American National Standards Institute Z39.48 Standard.
♻ This book was printed on 30% postconsumer recycled
paper. For more information please visit www.shambhala.com.

Distributed in the United States by Random House, Inc.,
and in Canada by Random House of Canada Ltd

Library of Congress Cataloging-in-Publication Data
Tipitaka, English. Selections.
The Buddha speaks/compiled and edited by
Anne Bancroft—1st ed.
p.   cm.
ISBN 978-1-57062-493-3 (cloth)
ISBN 978-1-59030-827-1 (paperback: alk. paper)
I. Bancroft, Anne, 1923– II. Title.
bq1172.e5 b36 2000   99-048885
294.3'82—dc21

CONTENTS

EDITOR'S PREFACE

This book presents the words of the Buddha as recorded by his followers. During the course of a long life spent traveling on foot between the villages and towns of north India, the Buddha (563–483 BCE) gave many discourses and much advice not only to his order of monks and nuns but also to kings and villagers, outcastes and thieves, for he did not recognize any caste boundaries.

The style of these discourses, when they came to be written down some three centuries later, was repetitive and often divided into numbered categories, for that was how the teachings had been memorized at a time when writing was rare and materials expensive. His followers would want to remember a sermon word for word, and a large body of material was preserved in this way. After the Buddha's death, the movement divided into two main schools, the Theravada and the Mahayana. The Theravada took Pali, an ancient Indian language, for its accounts of the Buddha's teach-ings, while the Mahayana expressed itself in the equally ancient and classical Sanskrit. As Bud-dhism spread to other countries, such as Korea, China, and Tibet, the original Pali or Sanskrit texts were translated into the native languages. This proved to be very fortunate, particularly with regard to the Sanskrit texts, for this preserved them from destruction by later invaders. The Pali texts survived more easily because King Ashoka (third century BCE) of India, a keen Buddhist, had them written in document form as well as inscrib-ing them on stones throughout the country.

In the late nineteenth century, translations were made of the Pali texts into European languages, and the translators—notably the Pali Text Soci-ety—followed the original words very closely. A little later the Sanskrit texts, too, began to be translated, and the chief English translator was Professor Edward Conze.

The Pali texts in particular have remained rather impenetrable because their late-Victorian translators not only kept to the original repetitive style but also used phrases and words of their own time that today have become obscure. Neverthe-less, the essential Buddha, the brilliant teacher and philosopher who never claimed to be anything more than a human being, shines through, and there are constant intimations of a wonderful mind—wise and serene, yet full of energy and humor; strongly compassionate, yet practical and penetratingly sane.

The central message of the Buddha was that every single one of us can find freedom from the deluded servitude that binds us to desires and cravings. By contemplation we can observe how life is. With awareness we can understand correctly the way to live and find clarity within confusion or despair. When we see the interconnectedness of all existence, we can free ourselves from self-love and the narrow confines of the self. Once the self has lost its power, a new consciousness is experienced that is timeless and unconditioned. This is nirvana never apart from the world but only to be apprehended when the world is no longer clutched at. The Buddha's own account of his awakening to these truths forms the first passage in the book.

The extracts in this book have been carefully edited to keep to the original text as closely as possible while at the same time using appropriate modern words and phrases instead of outdated ones. In this way the Buddha can speak to us as he spoke to the inhabitants of north India two and a half millennia ago. The reader will discover that the situations the Buddha came across in his many encounters with the people he met are intrinsically the same as the situations we find ourselves in today. His advice to his followers is as clear and necessary for our world as it was to theirs.

THE BUDDHA SPEAKS

# Awakening

When I was a young man, at the beginning of my life, I looked at nature and saw that all things are subject to decay and death and thus to sorrow. The thought came to me that I myself was of such a nature. I was the same as all created things. I too would be subject to disease, decay, death, and sorrow. But what if I were to search for that which underlies all becoming, for the unsurpassed perfect security which is nirvana, the perfect freedom of the unconditioned state?

So, in the first flush of my independence, I went against my father's wishes, shaved off my thick black hair, put on a saffron robe, and left my father's house for a homeless life. I wandered a long time, searching for what is good, searching after an unsurpassed state of peace.

At last I came to a pleasant forest grove next to a river of pure water and sat down beneath a big tree, sure that this was the right place for realization.

All the conditions of the world came into my mind, one after another, and as they came they were penetrated and put down. In this way, finally, a knowledge and insight arose, and I knew that this was the changeless, the unconditioned. This was freedom.

The reality that came to me is profound and hard to see or understand because it is beyond the sphere of thinking. It is sublime and unequaled but subtle and only to be found by the dedicated.

Most people fail to see this reality, for they are attached to what they cling to, to pleasures and delights. Since all the world is so attached to material things, it's very difficult for people to grasp how everything originates in conditions and causes. It's a hard job for them to see the meaning of the fact that everything, including ourselves, depends on everything else and has no permanent self-existence.

If I were to try to teach this truth, this reality, nobody would understand me, I thought. My labor and my trouble would be for nothing.

But then it came to me as an insight that I should teach this truth, for it is also happiness. There are people whose sight is only a little clouded, and they are suffering through not hearing the reality. They would become knowers of the truth.

It was in this way I went forth to teach:

For those who are ready, the door
To the deathless state is open.
You that have ears, give up
The conditions that bind you, and enter in.

Majjhima Nikaya

In all its parts, both small and infinite,
This one transcended his own life's history.
Composed and calm, he broke apart,
Like a shell of armor, all that makes the self.

Digha Nikaya

The mighty ocean has but one taste, the taste of salt.
Even so, the true way has but one savor, the savor of
freedom.

Majjhima Nikaya

Subhuti, does it occur to you that I believe that
through me living beings are led to liberation? Never
think that way, Subhuti. Why? Because there is no
separate being to lead to liberation. If I were to think
there was, I would be caught in the notion of a self or
a person or a life span.

Subhuti, what I call a self is essentially not a self in

the way that an ordinary person thinks of it. But neither do I think of anyone as an ordinary person. However, knowing the essence, I can use the name— ordinary person.

Diamond Sutra

Overcome your uncertainties and free yourself from dwelling on sorrow. If you delight in existence, you will become a guide to those who need you, revealing the path to many.

Sutta Nipata

The Buddha was meditating on the bank of a river. A brahman performing his worship rituals nearby had some unused cake and wanted to give it away. He went over to the Buddha but was put off when he saw the Buddha's shaven head—a sign of a nobody.

"What caste are you?" he asked.

"I am not a brahman, a prince, a farmer, or any other caste. I am one who understands how existence comes into being. Your question about caste is irrelevant."

"You seem a wise man and so I want to give you this offering of cake. I like to make offerings, for I feel they will bring me merit. Can you tell me what makes an offering effective for merit?"

The Buddha replied: "Since you are searching for an understanding, listen carefully. Don't ask about caste or riches but instead ask about conduct. Look at the flames of a fire. Where do they come from? From a piece of wood—and it doesn't matter what wood. In the same way, a wise person can come from wood of any sort. It is through firmness and restraint and a sense of truth that one becomes noble, not through caste.

"I will tell you who is worth offerings. It is the one who doesn't cling to life and who has seen where birth and death end. In the fullness of that state he has realized the way things are. His mind no longer seeks resting places. He sees the end of habit-chains. No more does he think of himself in terms of a self, and so there is nothing in him that can lead to bewilderment. He perceives all phenomena with clarity. That is the one who is worthy of offerings. That is where offerings are due."

Overwhelmed, the brahman held out his cake. "I have now met a being who understands everything completely, therefore my offering will be true. I ask you to accept my cake."

But the Buddha replied: "Now, brahman, I do not accept gifts for telling the truth. This is not the way with people of clear knowledge. Go and find a great saint who is perfect and is able to calm all anxieties.

That will be the right place for a man like yourself who is looking for merit. That is how a gift will be effective."

The brahman put away his cake. "You are worthy of a gift, for you have given one to me. It is unsurpassable and of immense fruitfulness."

He then went on his way to find a perfect saint.

Sutta Nipata

Like entrusting yourself to a brave man when
    greatly afraid,
By entrusting yourself to the awakening mind,
You will be swiftly liberated,
Even if you have made appalling errors.

Majjhima Nikaya

Just as space reaches everywhere, without discrimination, Just so the immaculate element, which in its essential nature is mind, is present in all.

Visuddhi Magga

If you really want freedom, happiness will arise
From happiness will come rapture

When your mind is enraptured, your body is
    tranquil
When your body is tranquil, you will know bliss
Because you are blissful, your mind will
    concentrate easily
Being concentrated, you will see things as they
    really are
In so seeing, you will become aware that life is a
    miracle
Being so aware, you will lose all your attachments
As you cease grasping, so you will be freed.

Digha Nikaya

The Buddha was instructing his monks: "Suppose there is a king who has never heard the sound of a lute. He hears it for the first time and exclaims, 'What is that beautiful sound?'

"His courtiers tell him it is the sound of a lute.

"'Bring me that lute,' he orders.

"But when he is given the lute he does not know what to do with it.

"'Take away the lute and just bring me that perfect sound.'

"'But we can't do that, Sire. There are many causes for that sound. There are all the parts of the lute, for one thing. The sound is made by the body and the sounding board, the arm, the head and strings, and the movement of the musician's fingers—'

"But the king could not understand that an entire system must be in place, and he broke the lute into pieces, saying: 'This lute has been deluding and deceiving people for too long.'

"Monks, we who look at the whole and not just the part, know that we too are systems of interdependence, of feelings, perceptions, thoughts, and consciousness all interconnected. Investigating in this way, we come to realize that there is no me or mine in any one part, just as a sound does not belong to any one part of the lute."

Samyutta Nikaya

The brahman Dona saw the Buddha sitting under a tree and was impressed by his peaceful air of alertness and his good looks. He asked the Buddha:

"Are you a god?"

"No, brahman, I am not a god."

"Then an angel?"

"No, indeed, brahman."

"A spirit, then?"

"No, I am not a spirit."

"Then what are you?"

"I am awake."

Anguttara Nikaya

"How can I tell that you are an enlightened person?" asked Sela the brahman of the Buddha.

"I know what should be known," answered the Buddha, "and what should be cultivated, I have cultivated. What should be abandoned, I have let go. In this way, O brahman, I am awake."

Sutta Nipata

You should do the work yourself, for buddhas only teach the way.

Dhammapada

Awake and rejoice in watchfulness. Understand the wisdom of the enlightened.

By watching keenly and working hard, the wise one may build himself an island which no flood can sweep away.

The thoughtless man does not care, but the attentive man looks on wakefulness as his greatest treasure.

Meditate, and in your wisdom realize nirvana, the highest happiness.

Dhammapada

There is freedom from desire and sorrow at the end of the way. The awakened one is free from all fetters and goes beyond life and death.

Like a swan that rises from the lake, with his thoughts at peace he moves onward, never looking back.

The one who understands the unreality of all things, and who has laid up no store—that one's track is unseen, as of birds in the air.

Like a bird in the air, he takes an invisible course, wanting nothing, storing nothing, knowing the emptiness of all things.

Dhammapada

At the moment of awakening, the Buddha exclaimed: "Wonder of wonders! All living beings are truly enlightened and shine with wisdom and virtue. But because their minds have become deluded and turned inward to the self, they fail to understand this."

Kegon Sutra

Subhuti, do not think that when one gives rise to the highest, most fulfilled, awakened mind one needs to see all objects of mind as nonexistent, cut off from life. Please do not think in that way. One who gives rise to the awakened mind does not deny objects or say that they are nonexistent.

One who gives rise to the awakened mind should

know that what is called a self or a person, a living being or a life span, is not so in essence but only in concept. The names *self, person, living being,* or *life span*
are names only. Subhuti, you should know that all the
things of the world are like this, and you should have
confidence in their essence without names.

As stars, a lamp, a fault of vision,
As dewdrops or a bubble,
A dream, a lightning flash, a cloud,
So one should see conditioned things.

Diamond Sutra

Subhuti asked: "Is perfect wisdom beyond thinking?
Is it unimaginable and totally unique but neverthe-
less reaching the unreachable and attaining the
unattainable?"

The Buddha replied: "Yes, Subhuti, it is exactly so.
And why is perfect wisdom beyond thinking? It is because all its points of reference cannot be thought
about but can be apprehended. One is the disappear-
ance of the self-conscious person into pure presence.
Another is the simple awakening to reality. Another
is the knowing of the essenceless essence of all things
in the world. And another is luminous knowledge
that knows without a knower. None of these points

can sustain ordinary thought because they are not objects or subjects. They can't be imagined or touched or approached in any way by any ordinary mode of consciousness, therefore they are beyond thinking."

Prajnaparamita

I declare that the overcoming of clinging to the impurities of the world is possible for a person who knows and sees but not for a person who does not know or see. In the person who knows and sees, the dustless and stainless Eye of Truth arises. Seeing the truth, he sees things as they are. Seeing the truth, the eye is born, knowledge is born, wisdom is born, science is born, and light is born.

Samyutta Nikaya

Ananda, the nature of the Absolute is that it is total enlightenment. It is beyond name and form and beyond the world and all its living beings. Ignorance creates an illusion of birth and death, but when ignorance is dispelled, the supreme and shining Absolute is there. Then, suffering is changed into insight, and death is transmuted into nirvana.

Surangama Sutra

 # LOVE

Putting down all barriers, let your mind be full of love. Let it pervade all the quarters of the world so that the whole wide world, above, below, and around, is pervaded with love. Let it be sublime and beyond measure so that it abounds everywhere.

Digha Nikaya

Of all the ways you can think of, none has a sixteenth part of the value of loving-kindness. Loving-kindness is a freedom of the heart which takes in all the ways. It is luminous, shining, blazing forth.

Just as the stars have not a sixteenth part of the moon's brilliance, which absorbs them all in its shining light, so loving-kindness absorbs all the other ways with its lustrous splendor.

Just as when the rainy season ends and the sun rises up into the clear and cloudless sky, banishing all the dark in its radiant light, and just as at the end of a black night the morning star shines out in glory, so none of the ways you can use to further your spiritual progress has a sixteenth part of the value of loving-kindness. For it absorbs them all, its luminosity shining forth.

Itivuttaka Sutta

This itself is the whole of the journey, opening your heart to that which is lovely. Because of their feeling for the lovely, beings who are afraid of birth and death, aging and decaying, are freed from their fear. This is the way you must train yourself: I will become a friend and an intimate of the lovely. To do this I must closely observe and embrace all states of mind that are good.

Samyutta Nikaya

The Buddha was told that his father, King Suddhodana, was getting old and anxious to see him. Consequently he traveled a long distance to his father's palace in Kapilavastu, taking two months for the journey and teaching on the way. His disciples went with him, and arrangements were made for the party to stay in the royal park when they arrived. But the court attendants looked down on the Buddha for giving up his princehood and becoming a homeless wanderer and they saw to it that no food was provided for his noonday meal, his only one of the day.

Untroubled, the Buddha took his begging bowl and went from house to house in Kapilavastu, his disciples with him. The king was told of this and hurried out to the Buddha, demanding to know why he was disgracing the family in this way. "To beg is the custom of our order," the Buddha told him.

The king was astonished. "But ours is a warrior lineage, and not a single warrior has ever gone out begging."

"The warrior lineage is yours, O King," answered the Buddha, "mine is the buddha lineage."

Standing in the street, he advised the king: "Be alert, be attentive. Lead a good life. The good live happily in this world and the next."

The king saw the truth of this. He took the bowl from the Buddha and led him and all the disciples to the palace, where he served them with food. From then on he lived a thoughtful and unpretentious life.

Digha Nikaya

When people speak badly of you, you should respond in this way: Keep a steady heart and don't reply with harsh words. Practice letting go of resentment and accepting that the other's hostility is the spur to your understanding. Be kind, adopt a generous standpoint, treat your enemy as a friend, and suffuse all your world with affectionate thoughts, far-reaching and widespread, limitless and free from hate. In this state you should try to remain.

Dhammapada

The Buddha was joined by his own son, Rahula, a young boy. He advised him: "Cultivate, Rahula, a meditation on loving-kindness, for by cultivating loving-kindness, ill will is banished forever. Cultivate, too, a meditation on compassion, for by cultivating compassion, you will find harm and cruelty disappear."

Majjhima Nikaya

A person who gives freely is loved by all. It's hard to understand, but it is by giving that we gain strength. But there is a proper time and proper way to give, and the person who understands this is strong and wise. By giving with a feeling of reverence for life, envy and anger are banished. A path to happiness is found. Like one who plants a sapling and in due course receives shade, flowers, and fruit, so the results of giving bring joy. The way there is through continuous acts of kindness so that the heart is strengthened by compassion and giving.

Majjhima Nikaya

A rich man said to the Buddha, "I see you are the Awakened One and I would like to open my mind to you and ask your advice. My life is full of work, and having made a great deal of money, I am surrounded by cares. I employ many people who depend on me to be successful. However, I enjoy my work and like working hard. But having heard your followers talk of the bliss of a hermit's life and seeing you as one who gave up a kingdom in order to become a homeless wanderer and find the truth, I wonder if I should do the same. I long to do what is right and to be a blessing to my people. Should I give up everything to find the truth?"

The Buddha replied: "The bliss of a truth-seeking life is attainable for anyone who follows the path of unselfishness. If you cling to your wealth, it is better to throw it away than let it poison your heart. But if you don't cling to it but use it wisely, then you will be a blessing to people. It's not wealth and power that enslave men but the clinging to wealth and power.

"My teaching does not require anyone to become homeless or resign the world unless he wants to, but it does require everyone to free himself from the illusion that he is a permanent self and to act with integrity while giving up his craving for pleasure.

"And whatever people do, whether in the world or as a recluse, let them put their whole heart into it. Let them be committed and energetic, and if they have to struggle, let them do it without envy or hatred. Let them live not a life of self but a life of truth, and in that way bliss will enter their hearts."

Majjhima Nikaya

In reply to the question, What is the best that people can possess, what brings them truest happiness, what is the sweetest of the sweet, and what is the pleasantest life to live? The Buddha answered:

"Trust is the best that people can possess; following the way brings truest happiness; truth is the sweetest of the sweet; and the practice of insight is the pleasantest way to live."

Sutta Nipata

Whatever living beings there may be—feeble or strong, small or large, seen or unseen, those who live far or those near, those who are born and those who are yet to be born—may all beings, without exception, experience a happy mind.

Let one not deceive another nor despise any person whatever in any place. In anger or ill will let one not wish any harm to another.

Let one's thoughts of boundless love pervade the whole world without any obstruction, without any hatred, without any enmity.

Samyutta Nikaya

A mother, even at the risk of her own life, protects her child, her only child. In the same way should you cultivate love without measure toward all beings. You should cultivate toward the whole world— above, below, around—a heart of love unstinted, un-mixed with any sense of differing or opposing interests. You should maintain this mindfulness all the time you are awake. Such a state of heart is the best in the world.

Majjhima Nikaya

It is in this way that we must train ourselves: by liber-ation of the self through love. We will develop love, we will practice it, we will make it both a way and a basis, take our stand upon it, store it up, and thor-oughly set it going.

Samyutta Nikaya

The Buddha had heard that his monks were quarreling among themselves. He told them a story:

"In Benares there was a powerful king, Brahmadatta, who went to war against Dirgheti, the king of Koshala, for he thought the kingdom of Koshala was small and an easy conquest. Dirgheti saw that resistance was useless and so he fled his kingdom and after much wandering reached Benares and lived there with his wife in a potter's dwelling. There they had a son and called him Dirghayu.

"When Dirghayu had grown up, Dirgheti thought to himself, Brahmadatta has done us great harm and will be fearing our revenge. If ever he finds us, he will kill us. So he sent Dirghayu, his son, away. Dirghayu finished his education and became skillful and wise.

"But Dirgheti's former barber, who lived in Benares, saw him one day and betrayed him to Brahmadatta for a reward. Brahmadatta had Dirgheti and his queen paraded through the streets, and there, to his horror, Dirgheti saw his son. Afraid he would draw attention to himself, he called out, 'Do not look at us. Turn away. Hatred is not appeased by hatred, only by forgiveness.' Then he and his wife were executed. But when night arrived, Dirghayu took their bodies and burned them on a funeral pyre with honors.

"Hearing of this, Brahmadatta was sure that Dirghayu would assassinate him if he could. But Dirghayu had gone to the forest, where he could be alone in his sorrow. After some time he returned to Benares, and hearing there was a job in the royal elephant stable, he took it. The king overheard him singing a sad but beautiful song to the accompaniment of his lute and was so touched by Dirghayu's sweet voice that he asked the young man to join his retinue. He soon saw how wise, good-tempered, and reliable Dirghayu was and gave him a position of trust.

"The king went hunting and took Dirghayu as his only companion. He became tired and lay down with his head in Dirghayu's lap. At last, here was Dirghayu's opportunity to avenge himself for the robbery of his kingdom and his parents' deaths. He unsheathed his sword. But then he remembered his father's last words to him, that hatred can never be appeased by hatred, and he put his sword back. The king woke and said, 'I dreamed that young Dirghayu was about to kill me with his sword.'

"Dirghayu laid one hand on the king's head and with the other took out his sword again. 'I am Dirghayu. The time of revenge has come.'

"The king saw that he was at his mercy, and said, 'Grant me my life, dear Dirghayu. Please grant me my life.'

"'How can I grant you your life when my life is in

danger from you? It is you who must grant me my life.'

"And the king said, 'I will grant you your life if you will grant me mine.'

"They took each other's hands and swore never to harm each other. Out of remorse, the king gave Dirghayu back his kingdom."

The Buddha ended his story with the comment: "Now, monks, if such can be the forbearance of kings who are used to ruling with the sword, so much more must you let your light shine before the world. You, having embraced the life of a seeker, must show yourselves to be forbearing and generous. No more altercations, no arguments, no disunion, no quarrels."

Udana Sutta

The one who practices loving-kindness sleeps and wakes in comfort and has no bad dreams; he is dear to both humans and creatures; no danger harms him. His mind can be quickly concentrated, his expression is happy and serene. He dies without any confusion of mind. Loving-kindness protects him.

Anguttara Nikaya

Be loving, be kind
And follow the ways of goodness.
Committed, and longing for the goal,
Always keep going with courage.
To dally and delay will not help you.
But to be ardent is sure and safe.
When you see it, cultivate the path,
So you will touch and make your own
The Deathless Way.

Psalms of the Early Buddhists

The one who gives himself entirely to sense pleasures and does not contemplate gives up the real for the pleasant. He comes to envy the one who pursues wisdom.

Do not cling to the pleasant, much less to the unpleasant. Losing that which you love brings suffering; harboring the pain of your loss brings more pain.

Dhammapada

Ananda, an attendant of the Buddha, passed by a well near a village. A young low-caste woman, Pakati, was fetching water. He asked her for a drink.

Pakati said: "I am low caste and therefore may not give you water. Please ask nothing from me in case I contaminate your holy state with my low-caste status."

Ananda said: "I am not interested in caste. It is water I am after."

Pakati's heart leaped joyfully. She gave him water to drink, and when he left she followed him at a discreet distance. Finding out that he was a disciple of the Buddha, she went to the Buddha and said, "Please accept me and let me live in this place where your disciple Ananda dwells, so that I may see him and supply him with what he needs. For I find that I love Ananda."

The Buddha understood what was going on in her feelings and he said gently, "Pakati, your heart is full of love but you don't understand your own emotions. It is not Ananda that you love, but his kindness. Accept the kindness that he has shown to you and in your turn practice it toward others. You have been born low caste, but in this way you will be a model for highborn nobles. Keep to this path and in time you will outshine the glory of kings and queens."

Agamas

Arouse your will, supreme and great,
Practice love, give joy and protection;

Let your giving be like space,
Without discrimination or limitation.

Do good things, not for your own sake
But for all the beings in the universe;
Save and make free everyone you encounter,
Help them attain the wisdom of the way.

Prajnaparamita

Ananda said to the Buddha: "I think there has never been a teacher as great as you, nor will there ever be one as great in the future."

The Buddha asked: "Have you known all the awakened ones, the buddhas of the past?"

"No, Honored One."

"And are you able to know all the buddhas of the future?"

"No, Honored One."

"Then I suppose you do know this awakened one's mind completely?"

"No, Honored One, I do not even know your mind completely."

"Then how can you make such a bold statement? It is better to talk of what you know than to speculate foolishly."

Majjhima Nikaya

All those who clearly understand the fact that enlightenment is everywhere come to the perfect wisdom with a marvelous insight that all objects and structures, just as they are in the present moment, are themselves enlightenment, both the way and the goal, being perfectly transparent to the ineffable. Those who experience the ineffable, known as Suchness, recognize that all structures are radiantly empty of self-existence.

Those who attain perfect wisdom are forever inspired by the conviction that the infinitely varied forms of this world, in all their relativity, far from being a hindrance and a dangerous distraction to the spiritual path, are really a healing medicine. Why? Because by the very fact that they are interdependent on each other and therefore have no separate self, they express the mystery and the energy of all-embracing love. Not just the illumined wise ones but every single being in the interconnected world is a dweller in the boundless infinity of love.

Prajnaparamita

 CLARITY

Subhuti asked the Buddha: "The highest, most awakened mind that you have attained—is that mind the unattainable?"

"Yes, Subhuti. With regard to that highest and most awakened mind, I have not attained anything. That mind is everywhere equally. It cannot be attained or grasped, but it can be realized. It is realized through the practice of all good actions when they are done in the spirit of no self and no object of self."

Prajnaparamita

A name is imposed on what is thought to be a thing or a state and this divides it from other things and other states. But when you pursue what lies behind the name, you find a greater and greater subtlety that has no divisions. Atoms of dust are not really atoms of dust but are merely called that. In the same way, a world is not a world but is merely called that.

Visuddhi Magga

Subhuti asked: "What does *buddha* mean?"

The Buddha answered: "Buddha is reality. One who thoroughly comprehends all the factors of existence is a buddha."

Then Subhuti asked: "What does *enlightenment* mean?"

The Buddha replied: "Enlightenment is a way of saying that all things are seen in their intrinsic empty nature, their Suchness, their ungraspable wonder. Names or words are merely incidental, but that state which sees no division, no duality, is enlightenment."

Subhuti asked: "If one wants to know emptiness, how should one do it?"

"The one who wants to realize emptiness should adore reality, develop a skill in living in the world, and cultivate friends of the same mind. Skill can only be developed in the presence of reality, not otherwise. Endowed with skill, the person gives without the idea of a giver and lives in the realization that all the factors of existence have no ultimate substance."

Prajnaparamita

The eye of clarity is so called because it brings sight to everyone. It enables every single one to enter the uncreated and unconditioned reality, each in his own way.

Prajnaparamita

What is not yours, put away; putting it away will be for your good and welfare. What are the things that are not yours? Your body is not yours—put it away. Your feelings come and go, don't own them, put them away. Perception and the things you perceive are not yours, put them down. The way your brain works and forms ideas is not yours, let it go. Consciousness is a condition that is general, it is not yours, do not own it. Letting go and putting away and not owning will be for your good and welfare.

Samyutta Nikaya

Just as the footprint of any creature that walks the earth can be placed in the elephant's footprint, which is the largest of all—even so mindful attention is the one quality that ensures ease of mind at all times.

Mindful attention causes beneficial thoughts that have not yet arisen to arise. It also causes harmful thoughts that have already arisen to vanish. In the one who is mindful, the good that is to be will be realized.

Anguttara Nikaya

The Buddha noticed Sigala, a householder, clasping his hands and then turning in the four directions as well as to the sky above and the earth beneath. The

Buddha knew this was a ritual to avert evil and he asked Sigala:

"Why do you perform this strange ceremony?"

"Do you think it strange that I should protect my home against the influence of demons? I know that you, O Buddha, believe that incantations are no use, but I know that in performing this rite I am honoring my father and keeping his instructions sacred."

"You do well, Sigala, to honor your father and keep his instructions. And it's your duty to protect your home and your family. I don't find anything wrong in your performing your father's ritual, but I don't think you understand the ceremony. Let me, as your spiritual father, explain:

"To guard your home by mysterious ceremonies is not enough, you must guard it by good deeds. With good deeds you should turn to your parents in the east, your teachers in the south, your wife and children in the west and your friends in the north. Above you, worship the spirit, and below you, honor all that serve you. That is the real protection your father wants you to have, and when you perform this ritual you will be reminded of it."

Then Sigala looked to the Buddha as his own father and said, "I never knew what I was doing but now I know."

Majjhima Nikaya

The brightly shining mind is never absent but is colored by the thoughts and emotions that people put upon it. If you were to see the luminous freedom of this mind, you would cultivate it before any other, keeping it free from all attachments.

Anguttara Nikaya

A soldier came to the Buddha and asked: "It is said that you deny the existence of the soul. Do those who say this speak the truth or are they bearing false witness against you?"

The Buddha replied: "There is a way in which they are speaking the truth; on the other hand, there is a way in which they are not. I teach that there is no separate reality that is the self. On the other hand, I do teach that there is perception. The one who understands soul as perceptive mind and says that perception exists teaches the truth that leads to clarity and enlightenment."

The soldier asked: "Do you then believe that two things exist? The world that we perceive with our senses, and the mind?"

The Buddha answered: "This is what I say: Your mind is spiritual and so too is the sense-perceived world. The spirit is timeless and it dominates all existence as the great law guiding all beings in their search for truth. It changes crude nature into mind, and there is no being that can't be transformed into a vessel of truth."

Brahmajala Sutra

To reflect on the beginning and end of things is to feel happiness as you see the boundless joy of worlds beyond worlds.

Look to your own perceptive mind, which is intrinsically pure, and rouse yourself. Look to the purity on which the world is founded and correct yourself. Look within and find happiness. Feel no more doubt.

When you are no longer dependent on name and form, you will indeed become a seeker.

You are the master and you are also the way. Where else can you look? As a merchant breaks in a noble horse, so you should master yourself.

The seeker who has confidence in the way will go beyond the way and find the end of suffering.

The seeker who goes beyond the way enlightens the world, just as the moon shines as it passes from behind the clouds.

Dhammapada

Different winds come from all directions. Some are clear, some carry dust, some are cold or hot, fierce gales or gentle breezes. In the same way sensations arise in the body—pleasant or unpleasant or neutral. When a meditator sees sensations as he does the winds, coming and going, clear or dust laden, fierce or gentle, he will fully understand them and be free from dependence on them. When he understands sensations perfectly, he will see beyond this conditioned world.

Samyutta Nikaya

Empty and calm and devoid of self
Is the nature of all things.
No individual being
In reality exists.

There is no end or beginning,
Nor any middle course.
All is illusion,
As in a vision or a dream.

All beings in the world
Are beyond the realm of words.
Their ultimate nature, pure and true,
Is like the infinity of space.

Prajnaparamita

The one whose mind knows the clarity of perfect wisdom is never afraid or even anxious. Why? Because when being at one with the living power of wisdom, the mother of all the buddhas, that person has the strength to remain in a state of undivided contemplation even while ceaselessly and skillfully engaging in compassionate action. The wise one is enabled to act because of concentration on a single prayer: "May all beings never leave the path of enlightenment, which is their own true nature and is empty of separate self-existence."

Prajnaparamita

The one who is very attached to the cave of the body, that one finds detachment very difficult. Those who constantly crave for pleasure are hard to liberate and certainly cannot be liberated by others, only by themselves. Sometimes it is only death that brings a realization of endings, and then the sensual person, deeply immersed in the body, will shout: "What will happen to me after death?"

The way toward liberation is to train yourself to live in the present without wanting to become anything. Give up becoming this or that, live without cravings, and experience this present moment with full attention. Then you will not cringe at death nor seek for repeated birth.

Sutta Nipata

A questioner asked the Buddha: "I would like to know about the state of peace, the state of solitude and of quiet detachment. How does a person become calm, independent, and not wanting to grasp at anything?"

"A person does this," replied the Buddha, "by eradicating the delusion of 'I am.' By being alert and attentive, he begins to let go of cravings as they arise. But whatever he begins to accomplish, he should beware of inner pride. He must avoid thinking of himself as better than another, or worse or equal, for that is all comparison and emphasizes the self.

"The person should look for peace within and not depend on it in any other place. For when a person is quiet within, the self cannot be found. There are no waves in the depths of the ocean, it is still and unbroken. It is the same with the peaceful person. He is still, without any longing to grasp. He has let go the foundations of self and no longer builds up pride and desire."

Sutta Nipata

I have taught the way without making any distinction between inner and outer teaching. For in respect of the truth there must be no such thing as the "closed fist" of the teacher, who hides some essential knowledge from the pupil. Secrecy is the mark of false doctrine.

Digha Nikaya

Magandiya asked the Buddha: "What is your view and what is your way of life and your future destiny?"

The Buddha answered: "Studying all the opinions that people hold fast to, I do not say, 'I declare this' or 'I declare that.' Observing all human opinions but not grasping them, I searched for the truth and found inward peace."

"But how would a wise person describe the inward peace you found without referring to one of the speculative systems, without taking up one of the human opinions you would not grasp?"

"One does not attain peace by speculation, tradition, knowledge, ritual, or viewpoint, but nor is it attained without the help of any of those. It is by taking those factors as means and not grasping them as ends in themselves that one finds peace and clarity."

"But if you say that clarity is not to be attained with tradition and viewpoint and yet is not attained by absence of these," persisted Magandiya, "then it seems to me that what you are talking is nonsense. Most people think that clarity comes from a viewpoint."

"It is because of your own fixed viewpoint that you keep on asking these questions," replied the Buddha, "You are obsessed with your preconceived notions and are holding on to them fast. I don't believe you've heard anything I've said; that's why you regard it as nonsense. You are looking for some superiority. But there are no such thoughts of superior or equal or inferior to one who has found clarity, because to think in that way is immediately to enter into disputation. Why should the wise person argue, saying 'This is truth' or 'This is a lie'? And if he has no such thoughts as equal or unequal, who is he going to dispute with?

"The one who wanders independent in the world, free from opinions and viewpoints, does not grasp them and enter into disputations and arguments. As the lotus rises on its stalk unsoiled by the mud and the water, so the wise one speaks of peace and is unstained by the opinions of the world."

Sutta Nipata

What is meant by nonduality, Mahatmi? It means that light and shade, long and short, black and white, can only be experienced in relation to each other; light is not independent of shade, nor black of white. There are no opposites, only relationships. In the same way, nirvana and the ordinary world of suffering are not two things but related to each other. There is no nirvana except where the world of suffering is; there is no world of suffering apart from nirvana. For existence is not mutually exclusive.

Lankavatara Sutra

The student Punnaka asked the Buddha: "Why is it that the wise men in the world—priests, rulers, and others—always offer sacrifices to the gods?"

The Buddha answered: "They offer things to the gods because as they get older they want to keep their lives as they are and have no misfortunes."

"But, Buddha," asked Punnaka, "does it ever make any difference to their old age by making these careful offerings?"

"Their prayers and praises and offerings and hopes are all made on the basis of possessions, rewards, and longings for pleasure. These experts in prayer are longing to continue becoming. But it will make no difference to their old age."

"Please tell me, Buddha, if all the offerings from these

experts don't get them beyond old age, then who has ever gone beyond?"

The Buddha said: "When a person has thoroughly understood the world, from top to bottom, when there is nothing in the world that agitates him anymore, then he has become somebody who is free from confusion and fears and tremblings and the longings of desire. He has gone beyond getting old and beyond birth and death."

Sutta Nipata

The Buddha was asked: "To what extent can a person be a speaker of the way?"

He answered. "If a person teaches the way in order to transcend the tyranny of material things and to teach how to transcend feelings, perceptions, impulses, and consciousness —teaching nonattachment with regard to these—then that person can be called a speaker of the way. If he is himself trying to transcend the pull of the material world and to feel nonattachment toward it, then it is fitting to say he is living in accordance with the way. If he is liberated by this transcendence and nonattachment, then you can say he has found nirvana here and now.

Samyutta Nikaya

Shariputra asked: "When a follower attains the great insight of perfect wisdom, does that follower then covet and cultivate omniscience, infinite knowledge?"

The Buddha answered: "Such a follower never covets or cultivates infinite knowledge. That very attitude of not coveting and not cultivating reveals everything to him and he sees all possible structures—from objects of the senses to buddhas—to be transparent in their nature. This radiant transparency is, in fact, simply the total awakeness of a buddha. The now-awakened follower becomes, in this way, immersed in infinite wisdom and blossoms spontaneously as omniscience itself."

Prajnaparamita

Describing his awakening, the Buddha said: "Coming to be, coming to be! Ceasing to be, ceasing to be! At that thought, monks, there arose in me a vision of things not before called to mind. Knowledge arose— such is form, such is the coming to be of form, such is its passing away. Recognition arose—such is its coming to be, such is its passing away. And the state of abiding in the understanding of arising and passing away—that too arose."

Samyutta Nikaya

# BODY AND MIND

Ananda said: "Friendship with what is lovely, association with what is lovely, intimacy with what is lovely—that is half of the holy life."

The Buddha responded: "Don't say that, Ananda. It's the whole not the half of the holy life. One so blessed with what is lovely will develop a right way of being, a thinking that no longer grasps at what is untrue, an aim that is concerned and ready, a contemplation that is unattached and free. Association with what is lovely is the whole of the holy life."

Samyutta Nikaya

Rohitassa asked: "Is there anywhere, while one is continuing on the path, where one can find a place where there is no birth, no aging, no decaying, no ending, and no rising again in rebirth? Is there anywhere along the way where one can see the end or reach the end of existence?"

"No, my friend," replied the Buddha, "there is nowhere of that nature. When you are following the path, you can't know the end or see the end or reach the end of existence. But, nevertheless, you can end your trouble and woe—indeed, you can end it here and now. For in this very body, six feet in length, with all its sense impressions and its thoughts and ideas, here I declare to you is the world and the origin of the world and the ending of the world and also the way that leads to that ending."

> Not to be reached by traveling is the end of the
>   world,
> Yet there is no release from sorrow
> Unless you reach the end of the world.
> The one who is wise and lives a loving life
> Begins to know the world. That one will go to the
>   world's end.
> And then he will neither long for this world
> Nor for any world.
>
> *Anguttara Nikaya*

I will teach you the All. Listen closely. What is the All? It is eye and visible object, ear and sound, nose and scent, tongue and taste, body and feelings, mind and ideas. This is the All.

If anyone says, "This All is not enough. I will proclaim another All," can it be done? The speaker might believe it can, but he will not be able to show another All.

Samyutta Nikaya

In the Himalayas there is land that is rough and hard to cross, where neither monkeys nor humans can live. And there is other land where monkeys can live but not humans. As well, there are delightful valleys where both monkeys and humans can live.

In these valleys, hunters set traps of sticky pitch among the monkeys' trees to catch them. The monkey who is free from curiosity and greed, when it sees the pitch trap stays away from it. But a foolish and greedy monkey will come up to the pitch and handle it with his paw. His paw will then stick fast. He will seize it with the other paw, but then that too will stick. To free both of them, he tries to use his feet, but when they too are captured, he uses his mouth. When that sticks he is caught in all five ways, so he lies down and howls. The hunter hears the howl and comes to finish him off.

It is the same for one who wanders in the wrong places. What are the wrong places? Attaching oneself to the delights of the five senses and being trapped and enslaved by that delight, that is the wrong place; that enslavement is beyond the needs and the range of a life.

You should roam in places that are your own, that arise in accordance with your true nature.

And what is the place that is your own? It's the pasture of ardent clearness and mindfulness, where discontent and greed are put aside for the sake of the world. That is your own place, your natural range.

Samyutta Nikaya

There is a universal condition which I have penetrated and realized. Having realized it, I can now declare it, teach it, and define it, opening it up for all to understand.

What is this world condition?

Body is the world condition. And with body and form goes feeling, perception, consciousness, and all the activities throughout the world. The arising of form and the ceasing of form—everything that has been heard, sensed, and known, sought after and reached by the mind—all this is the embodied world, to be penetrated and realized.

Samyutta Nikaya

The jasmine has put forth fresh blooms today,
Dropping yesterday's withered flowers.
So let drop your old lusts and hates.

Serene in body, speech, and mind,
When all the world's cravings are set aside,
You will know yourself as tranquil.

Rouse yourself to examine yourself,
Be watchful and intent,
Guard this self and live happily.

Dhammapada

When causes and conditions are sufficient, eyes are present. When causes and conditions are not sufficient, eyes are absent. The same is true of body and consciousness, mind and perception.

Diamond Sutra

Let me tell you about the middle path. Dressing in rough and dirty garments, letting your hair grow matted, abstaining from eating any meat or fish, does not cleanse the one who is deluded. Mortifying the flesh through excessive hardship does not lead to a triumph over the senses. All self-inflicted suffering is useless as long as the feeling of self is dominant.

You should lose your involvement with yourself and then eat and drink naturally, according to the needs of your body. Attachment to your appetites—whether you deprive or indulge them—can lead to slavery, but satisfying the needs of daily life is not wrong. Indeed, to keep a body in good health is a duty, for otherwise the mind will not stay strong and clear.

This is the middle path.

Discourse II

That people are unknowing does not mean that they are unknowing like cows or goats. Even ignorant people look for a pathway to reality. But, searching for it, they often misunderstand what they encounter. They pursue names and categories instead of going beyond the name to that which is real.

Digha Nikaya

One day a bright and intelligent disciple of the Buddha asked if he could fetch his younger brother to join the order. Delighted, the Buddha agreed.

But the younger brother, although kind and gentle, turned out to be slow and dull witted. He could un-

derstand nothing of his studies and asked to go home
so that he wouldn't waste the Buddha's time or let
down his brother.

"There's no need for you to give up," said the Buddha. "You should not abandon your search for liberation just because you seem to yourself to be thick
witted. You can drop all the philosophy you've been
given and repeat a mantra instead — one that I will
now give you." He gave the young monk a mantra and
sent him away affectionately.

But soon the monk was back, this time even more
humiliated. "My beloved Buddha, I can't remember the
mantra you gave me and so I can no longer practice."

The Buddha kindly repeated it for him. But twice
more he came back, having forgotten it each time. So
the Buddha gave him a simplified form. But when
this too slipped completely out of his mind, he hardly
dared visit the Buddha again.

"There's an even shorter version," the Buddha told
him, with a smile, "It's just two syllables. See if you
can remember that."

But he could not. In his hut, he broke down and
wept. His brother found him and was furious, feeling
that his own reputation was now sullied. He told the
young monk to go home, and so the boy left the hut
and sadly made his way along the path.

As he neared a grove of trees, he met the Buddha

coming from it. The Buddha smiled and took his hand. Together they went to a temple where two old monks were sweeping the floor. The Buddha said to them: "This young monk will live here with you from now on. Continue your sweeping, and as your brooms move back and forth, say the two-syllable mantra that I will now give you. Don't stop until I come back."

The young monk sat down and listened to the movement of the brooms, to and fro over the floor. He heard the whispered rhythm of the mantra as it was repeated over and over again. This went on for many weeks, and before the Buddha came back, the young monk had found full liberation and so had the two old monks.

Majjhima Nikaya

Since your mind is not physical,
No one else can destroy it.
But because of its attachments to the body,
It is harmed by physical suffering.

Bodhicharyavatara

A Jain argued with the Buddha: "You say that all things are changing and therefore have no permanent self. But plants depend on the earth for their growth, and in the same way a person is material and has needs and feelings and so on. So I say that this material shape and everything to do with it is my self."

"Do you have the power, then, to change your shape so that it is taller or shorter?" asked the Buddha.

"No," the Jain admitted.

"Are material objects permanent?"

"No."

"Is it wise then to think of impermanent material objects, such as your shape, as belonging to you or as yourself?"

"No, that would be wrong," said the Jain, "and I'm sorry if I spoke in an aggressive way. How do your disciples come to reach your understanding?"

"Having directly seen and realized all things, even thoughts and emotions, as they really are, they are able to say: 'This is not mine, this is not me, this is not myself.' In this way they are freed from their deluded attachment to themselves."

Majjhima Nikaya

The world is apprehended by way of the mind
The world is acted upon by way of the mind
And all good things and bad
Exist in the world by way of the mind.

Samyutta Nikaya

A brahman named Sangarava bathed every morning and evening in the river so that he could be cleansed from whatever sin he might have committed during the day.

To him, the Buddha said: "If bathing could purify one from sins, then all the frogs, turtles, and crocodiles would be free from sin! The real lake is the lake of goodness, with grace as its shore for bathing. Clear and undefiled, it soothes all who immerse themselves. Plunge into the waters of goodness and learn to swim."

Samyutta Nikaya

This body is not yours, nor does it belong to others. It should be seen as the product of the whole of history. In regard to it the wise person will reflect on the nature of conditioning, saying: If this comes into being, that will arise; if this does not come into being, that will not arise.

Samyutta Nikaya

There are two kinds of happiness. There is that of an uncommitted life of sensual pleasures, and there is that of a committed life, one of going forth to a new consciousness. Of these, the happiness of going forth is greater.

Anguttara Nikaya

The Buddha was talking with Uttara, the young pupil of a teacher called Parasariya.

"Uttara, does Parasariya teach you how to control your senses?"

"Yes, Buddha, he does teach us how to control our senses."

"How does he do this?"

"We are taught not to see material forms with the eye nor hear sounds with the ear. That is how to control the senses."

"But in that case, Uttara, the blind and the deaf must be in total control of their senses, for the one does not see and the other doesn't hear."

Uttara was silent.

"Well, Uttara, Parasariya teaches you one way and here we teach a different way. Let me tell you what we teach. When a monk sees a form with the eye, usually a feeling of liking or disliking comes into being. The monk then understands that liking or disliking has arisen but that either one is not inevitable but is conditioned and dependent on causes. So he heads for a state in which there is equanimity and finds that in so doing the liking or disliking has vanished and he sees things as they are. That is how he controls his senses. That is what we teach."

Majjhima Nikaya

Those people who conceive of a self see it usually in one of several ways. They think of the body as the self, or as the self having a body, or they see the body as part of the self, or the self as included in the body. But in all these ways the feeling of "I am" is never abandoned, for people do not see the arising and falling and the way of conditions but regard the body and self as solid entities.

Sutta Nipata

A comfort-loving monk named Sona was making violent efforts to become physically and mentally vigorous. But he seemed so unsuccessful that the thought came to him: My family is wealthy, perhaps I can enjoy my riches and yet do good. What if I were to give up the training and return to a rich but worthy life?

The Buddha knew what was going on in his head.

"Sona, were you not skillful at playing the lute when you were a layman?"

"Yes, Buddha."

"And what do you think, Sona, was it possible to play in tune when the lute was overstrung?"

"No, indeed, Buddha."

"And what do you think, Sona—suppose the strings were too slack, could you play it then?"

"No, indeed, Buddha."

"But when they were neither overstrung nor slack but keyed to the middle pitch, could you then play it?"

"Certainly, Buddha."

"Then, Sona, take heed that when effort is too strenuous it leads to strain and when too slack to laziness. So make a firm determination that you will adopt the middle way, not allowing yourself to struggle or to slacken, but recognizing that faith, energy, mindfulness, concentration, and wisdom are the fruits of a calm and equable middle way."

Sona followed this advice and in due course was awakened.

Theragatha

This mind is like a fish out of water that thrashes and throws itself about, its thoughts following each of its cravings.

Such a wandering mind is weak and unsteady, attracted here, there, and everywhere. How good it is to control it and know the happiness of freedom.

And yet how unruly still, how subtle the delusion of the thoughts. To quiet them and master them is the true way of happiness.

Putting a bridle on the wandering mind, single-mindedly the seeker halts his thoughts. He ends their darting waywardness and finds peace.

Dhammapada

It is hard to be born as a human being and hard to live the life of one. It is even harder to hear of the path and harder still to awake, to rise, and to follow.

Yet the teaching is simple: "Cease to do evil, learn to do good. And purify your mind.

"Hurt none by word or deed. Be moderate in your eating. Live in inner solitude. And seek the deepest consciousness." This is the teaching.

Dhammapada

Your perceptive mind is already luminous and shining brightly. But you color it with all your attachments. It is not easy to understand this, and many do not. They do not cultivate their perceptive mind. But that mind, luminous and brightly shining, is fundamentally free of all attachments, because they come and go. This you should understand and for you there should be cultivation of the perceptive mind.

Anguttara Nikaya

The body, monks, is not a self. The body has evolved out of time immemorial from causes and preconditions that are also without a self. How then could the body, evolving out of something that is not a self, be a self? The same is true of thoughts and ideas that have come into existence by the influence of all beings throughout time—how could thoughts and ideas be a self? So, too, with feelings and perceptions, which are relative to the body and mind— how could they be a self?

Samyutta Nikaya

When a lute is played, there is no previous store of playing that it comes from. When the music stops, it does not go anywhere else. It came into existence by way of the structure of the lute and the playing of the performer. When the playing ceases, the music goes out of existence.

In the same way all the components of being, both material and nonmaterial, come into existence, play their part, and pass away.

That which we call a person is the bringing together of components and their actions with each other. It is impossible to find a permanent self there. And yet there is a paradox. For there is a path to follow and there is walking to be done, and yet there is no walker. There are actions but there is no actor. The air moves but there is no wind. The idea of a specific self is a mistake. Existence is clarity and emptiness.

Visuddhi Magga

If your mind becomes firm like a rock
And no longer shakes
In a world where everything is shaking,
Your mind will be your greatest friend
And suffering will not come your way

Theragatha

CONTEMPLATION

Who will transcend this world? Who will transcend the realm of the dead, and heaven, too, with all its gods? Who will find the true and shining way of the path?

You will. Even as the gatherer of flowers discovers the finest and rarest, so you will gather the teachings and transcend this world.

When you know that the body is merely the foam on the crest of a wave, unreal as a mirage, you will break the flowery arrows of craving. Unseen, you will escape the king of death and travel onward.

The scent of sandalwood, lilies, and jasmine cannot travel against the wind, but you will travel. The fragrance of good works travels in all directions, even to the ends of the earth.

How brightly the lotus grows in the rubbish by the wayside. Its sweet scent lightens the heart.

So you, the awakened, will shine in the darkness

around you, spreading the sweet scent of your wisdom.

Dhammapada

Find a place where you are alone. Train yourself in the following way: When you breathe in, experience breathing in. When you breathe out, be fully conscious that you are breathing out. If you cherish and practice this, it will bear great fruit. Whatever you are doing and wherever you are, you will find steadiness, calm, and concentration if you become conscious of your breathing.

Majjhima Nikaya

Develop a meditation that is like water. Doing this, you will find that the thoughts and impressions that possess you will flow away. Just as people wash away their body liquids, their sweat and spittle, pus and blood, and yet the water is not troubled or disgusted— so this water meditation will bring you peace.

Majjhima Nikaya

A puzzled man asked the Buddha: "I have heard that some monks meditate with expectations, others meditate with no expectations, and yet others are indifferent to the result. What is the best?"

The Buddha answered: "Whether they meditate with or without expectations, if they have the wrong ideas and the wrong methods, they will not get any fruit from their meditation. Think about it. Suppose a man wants to have some oil and he puts sand into a bowl and then sprinkles it with salt. However much he presses it, he will not get oil, for that is not the method. Another man is in need of milk. He starts pulling the horns of a young cow. Whether he has any expectations or not, he will not get any milk out of the horn, for that's not the method. Or if a man fills a jar with water and churns it in order to get butter, he will be left only with water.

"But if somebody meditates with a wholesome attitude, with right attention and mindfulness, then whether he has expectations or not he will gain insight. It's like filling a bowl with oil seeds and pressing them or milking a cow by pulling the udder or filling a jar with cream and churning it. It's the right method."

Majjhima Nikaya

This is how you should contemplate. The world is an idea in the mind to which the word *world* has been attached. Beyond this idea is the mystery of beingness. But it's not possible to free people from their attachment to the idea—to that which blinds them to the reality—without appropriate methods. So you should tread the path of perfect giving, of patience, energy, meditation, and wisdom. Yet while following these activities, you should remain aware that the world is illusory. It is for the sake of those who do not know that you engage in dynamic and vigorous work and also in meditation and one-pointed attention. Understanding that without wisdom you can do nothing for others, you remain in the perfection of wisdom, which is the awareness that what you are doing is both essential and illusory.

Prajnaparamita

It is necessary to cultivate some discipline of mind, for an undisciplined mind always finds excuses to act selfishly and thoughtlessly. When the mind is undisciplined, the body is also undisciplined, and so is speech and action.

Anguttara Nikaya

Subhuti said: "If I understand correctly, one who wishes to reach perfect wisdom should study the way things are in the world and should practice the perfections fully and in depth but should not believe them to be ultimately real, nor should he make concepts and doctrines out of them."

The Buddha replied: "Just so, Subhuti. The one who contemplates existence in this way knows the nature of the conditioned and of the unconditioned and makes himself an expert in pointing out the truth to others, both with words and without words."

Subhuti asked: "But is this just for the wise and the intelligent?"

"No, indeed," replied the Buddha. 'This is open to all, even to the dull witted and to those who can't pay attention. The door is open to anyone who wants to tread this path—but not to the person who is lazy and indifferent."

Prajnaparamita

Fleeting is this world
Growth and decay its very nature
Things spring to being and again they cease
Happy the marvel of them and the peace.

Nidana Vagga

When you are thinking about an object, it sometimes occurs that evil, unwholesome thoughts connected with hate and delusion come into your mind. The way to get rid of them is to concentrate on another object that is wholesome and good. Just as a skilled carpenter knocks out a coarse peg with a fine one, so the evil thoughts will disappear. With their departure, the mind will become calm, unified, and concentrated once more.

Majjhima Nikaya

This is the path itself,
For none other leads
To purity of vision.
If you follow it,
Your suffering will come to an end.
Since I have learned how to remove
The thorns of delusions, I have revealed the path.
You yourself should always strive.
Buddhas only teach.
Those who walk in contemplation
Free themselves from bondage to themselves.

Dhammapada

The Buddha said to his monks: "It is the rainy season and I wish to live in solitude for these three months. I would like my only visitor to be the one who brings me food."

At the end of three months, he said:

"Monks, if those of other faiths were to ask you, 'What meditation did the Buddha practice during the rains?' you should say, 'He spent the rains practicing the meditation of mindfulness on the in and the out breath.' It was in this way, monks, that mindfully I breathed in and mindfully I breathed out. When breathing a long breath, I knew that it was long; and when breathing it out I knew 'I breathe out a long breath.' The same with the short breath, knowing it to be entering and knowing it to be leaving. In mindfulness I was conscious of the entire process.

"In this way also I practiced contemplation on the body. When standing, I was aware that I was standing; when sitting, there was total knowledge of sitting; and when lying down, the full experience of lying down. By experiencing each moment, my mind clung no more to the world.

"The mindfulness of in and out breathing, of body contemplation, of keeping consciousness of the moment, is a noble occupation and a sublime way, leading to independence of mind and to wisdom."

Samyutta Nikaya

Reality as it is becomes the right view of the meditator. Thinking of it as it is becomes the right thought. Awareness of it as it is becomes the right awareness. Concentration on it as it is becomes the right concentration. Actions of body and speech are then aligned to reality as it is. In this way the meditator develops and is fulfilled.

Majjhima Nikaya

One of the Buddha's monks, Purna, wanted to teach meditation to the Western Suner, a wild and dangerous people. The Buddha thought such an idea was overzealous but tested Purna.

"But, Purna, these are violent, cruel, and furious people. When they get angry and curse you, what will you think?"

"I shall think that they are basically kind and good although they address me with insults. And at least they don't beat me or stone me."

"But suppose they do beat you and hit you with stones, what will you think?"

"I shall think they are kind and good since at least they are not using clubs and swords."

"And if they do attack you with clubs and swords?"

"I shall still think they are kind and good for delivering me from this unfortunate body."

"Oh, very well, very well, Purna. With such perfect and saintly patience as all that you may certainly go and live among these violent people. Go, Purna—who knows, you may be able to deliver some and show them the way to freedom."

Majjhima Nikaya

One should not imagine oneself to be one with the eye or independent of it or the owner of it. The same with the ear and all the other senses, including the mind. Nor should one imagine oneself to be identical with the world or contained in it or independent of it or the owner of it.

In this way, free from imagining, one no longer clings to the things of the world. When one no longer clings, there is no more agitation, insecurity, and worry. Being no longer worried, one can reach into the depths of oneself and understand that where there has been loss there is now fulfillment.

Samyutta Nikaya

The one who wishes to escape from doubt
Should be attentive and alert;
Looking at mind and body both,
He should see the causes and the origins.

Patisambhida Magga

In the gloom and darkness of the night, when there is a sudden flash of light, a person will recognize objects; in the same way, the one with a flash of insight sees according to reality—"This is how sorrow works; this is how it arises; this is how it can come to an end; this is the path leading to that end."

Anguttara Nikaya

When you contemplate the body by being within the body, you should not engage in all sorts of ideas about it; the same when you contemplate feelings by being within feelings, you should enter in without ideas; the same applies to contemplating the mind by being within the mind and contemplating thoughts by being within thoughts. The thoughts should be just the objects of mind and you should not apply yourself to any train of ideas connected with them. In this way, by putting ideas aside, your mind will become tranquil and fixed on one point. It will then enter into a meditation that is without discursive thought and is rapturous and joyful.

Majjhima Nikaya

Subhuti, all seekers of the truth should give rise to a pure and clear intention. When they give rise to this intention, they should do it in this spirit: They should not rely on forms, sounds, smells, touchables, or objects of mind. They should give rise to an intention with their minds not dwelling anywhere.

Diamond Sutra

Subhuti asked: "How can the practitioner who wishes to help all beings find enlightenment awaken to the complete and perfect wisdom?"

The Buddha said: "This most subtle awakening comes about through moment-to-moment attentiveness. By way of attentiveness, there is attunement to the ways in which things manifest, such as form and consciousness. The practitioner awakens to perfect wisdom by becoming blissfully free from obsessions with habits, names, sense experiences, personal feelings, and with dread of dying and all the despair that goes with it.

"Free to experience all the rising of manifestation and its interdependent functioning without believing it to be the final reality, the practitioner avoids two fundamental errors—that this relative world is rooted on any solid foundation, and the opposite error that the manifest forms we see are mere illusions without proper physical and moral implications for every single mind-flow."

Prajnaparamita

"Shariputra, does it occur to any of my followers to think that after they have known full enlightenment they should lead all beings to nirvana?"

"No, Honored One."

"But that should be their intention. They should not be too caught up with themselves to believe that. A glowworm or firefly does not think that its light could illuminate the continent of India or even radiate over it. In the same way, the followers do not think that they can, after obtaining full enlightenment, lead all beings to nirvana. But the sun, when it has risen, radiates its light over the whole of India. Just so, an awakened follower when he is fully enlightened, without even consciously attempting to, leads all beings to nirvana."

Prajnaparamita

The sun shines by day, and the sage in his wisdom shines. The moon shines by night, and the sage shines in contemplation. But day and night, the enlightened shine in radiance of the spirit.

Dhammapada

Dhotaka asked the Buddha: "I so much want to hear you speak. Please, Master Teacher, explain to me: can a student who follows your teachings find the bliss of nirvana?"

"Any student who follows my teaching," answered the Buddha, "can find the bliss of nirvana if he really wants to do so, and if he is free from concepts and aware of the way things are."

"There is here in front of me," said Dhotaka, bowing down, "a man who has nothing but who sees everything. I honor you, sir. Please free me from confusion."

"It is not my practice to free anyone from confusion," answered the Buddha. "When you have understood the most valuable teachings, then you yourself will be able to cross that ocean."

"Have pity on me. Please teach me the way of detachment, so that I can know things as they are, so that I can begin to live in the peace and independence that will free me as if I lived in air."

"I will explain that peace which is not based on concepts and expectations, and which is attainable here and now. When you understand this peace you will find that your hold on the world is released.

"In every direction," said the Buddha, "above, below, around, and within, you see things you know and recognize. Put them down. Do not let consciousness dwell on the products of existence and things that come and go, for there is no rest or relief there. When you understand that by taking the objects of the world for granted as total reality, you are tied to the world, then this understanding will release you from your dependence on objects and will stop your craving and your desire for constant becoming. Then you can let go your hold and engage with things as they are, instead."

Sutta Nipata

Hearing the above, another questioner, Jatukkani, asked: "Like the sun which controls the world with its heat and light, you, Master, seem to control desire and pleasure. I have only a little understanding. How can I find and know the way to give up this world of birth and aging?"

The Buddha answered: "Lose your greed for pleasure. See how letting go of the world brings deep tranquillity. There is nothing you need hold on to and nothing you need push away. Live in the present but do not cling to it and then you can go from place to place in peace. There is a state of greed that enters and dominates the individual. But when that greed has gone, it is like poison leaving a body and death will have no more terror for you."

Sutta Nipata

A student asked: "For all the different people who have come to listen to your words, please tell us about the way you have found and known."

The Buddha answered: "When you take things it is because of a thirst, a clinging, and a grasping. You should lose that and lose it altogether, above, below, around, and within. It makes no difference what it is you are grasping. When you grasp, you are losing your freedom. Realize this and grasp at nothing. Then you will cease being a creature of attachment, tied to the power of death."

Sutta Nipata

Hearing the above, another questioner, Upashiva, asked the Buddha: "It is not possible for me to cross that great ocean of desire without help. Please tell me what things would help me to find my way across."

The Buddha told him: "There are two things you can use to help you cross. One is the perception that emptiness exists, and the other is the awareness that in fact all things are empty and wonderful."

"Great Teacher," said Upashiva, "when one is free from attachment and craving, when everything is let go and one depends on emptiness, will one be permanently in that state?"

"When you are free from craving for sense pleasures

and when you are aware of emptiness, you are free in a supreme way and that will not change. It is like a flame struck by a gust of wind. In a flash the flame has gone out. Similarly, the person is suddenly free and no more words can be said. When all the ways of being a self are let go and when all phenomena are seen to be empty, then all the ways of describing this have also vanished."

Sutta Nipata

Meditate on that which is beyond words and symbols. Forsake the demands of the self. By such forsaking you will live serenely.

Sutta Nipata

 SORROW

"Is suffering brought about by myself alone, good Buddha?" asked Kassapa.

"No, Kassapa."

"Then by another?"

"No, Kassapa."

"Then both together, myself and another?"

"No, Kassapa."

"Then is it brought about by chance?"

"No, Kassapa."

"Then is there no suffering?"

"No, Kassapa, it is not that there is no suffering. For there *is* suffering."

"Well then, perhaps you neither know nor see it, Buddha."

"It is not that I don't know suffering or don't see it. I know it well and see it."

"But to all my questions, good Buddha, you have answered no—and yet you say you know suffering and see it. Please teach me about it."

"Kassapa, there are two wrong views. One says that oneself is the entire author of a deed and all consequent suffering one brings upon oneself and this is so from the beginning of time. The other says that it is deeds by other people that bring about one's own suffering.

"You should avoid both these views, Kassapa. Here we teach another way. All deeds, whether your own or another's, are conditioned by ignorance and that is the origin of this whole mass of suffering. By ending that ignorance in yourself, and by way of yourself in others, wisdom comes into being and the suffering ceases."

Samyutta Nikaya

In a gabled house the rafters all converge on the ridgepole, they are fixed on the ridgepole and join together there equally; in the same way, whatever wrong states of mind exist, they are all rooted in ignorance, fixed in ignorance and joined together there. Ignorance of good is the cause of wrongdoing. Therefore, you must live in mindfulness and train yourself in this.

Samyutta Nikaya

As a tree with strong uninjured roots, though cut down, grows up again, so, when deep craving is not rooted out, suffering arises again and again.

Dhammapada

The noble path is the best of all paths, freedom from craving is the best state, and the one who has eyes to see is the happiest person.

The noble path is the way that leads to freedom from delusion, that leads to clarity.

The one who sees this path and follows it comes to the end of sorrow.

You yourself must make the effort; the awakened only point the way. Those who have entered the path and who meditate free themselves from the bonds of illusion.

Everything is changing. It arises and passes away. The one who realizes this is freed from sorrow. This is the shining path.

To exist is to know suffering. Realize this and be free from suffering. This is the radiant path.

There is no separate self to suffer. The one who understands this is free. This is the path of clarity.

Dhammapada

Those who are afraid of all the sufferings in the world, and yet who are afraid of death, seek for nirvana. But they do not know that the world and death and nirvana are not to be separated from one another. They imagine that nirvana is to be found through annihilation of the senses, not knowing that the world of the senses is already a mirage or a miracle when it is no longer clutched at.

Lankavatara Sutra

There is no fire like greed and no crime like hatred. There is no sorrow like being bound to this world; there is no happiness like freedom.

Health is the greatest of blessings, contentment the best of riches; trust is the best of relationships; nirvana is the highest happiness.

Having tasted the sweetness of inner solitude and contentment, he who lives by the law of the universe is free from fear and suffering.

It is joy to see such awakened ones, and to live with them is happiness.

To travel with fools makes the journey long and hard and is as painful as traveling with an enemy. But the company of the wise is as pleasant as meeting with friends.

Follow the wise, the intelligent, and the awakened.
Follow them as the moon follows the path of the stars.

Dhammapada

If you want to get rid of your enemy, the true way is to
realize that your enemy is delusion.

Kegon Sutra

Subhuti asked the Buddha in what way things, which
seem to be solid and separate, really exist.

The Buddha said: "Their true existence is free
from the illusion of self. The appearance of things
and events seeming to be solid and separate is the result of ignorance, which projects the idea of individ-
uality on the world. People who believe that all they
encounter and all that goes on in their minds is liter-
ally and totally true are trying to root themselves in
name and form and conventional ideas, and in conse-
quence they suffer. They go along with the false idea
that in order to exist at all a structure must be material. This false reasoning blinds them to the transparent, insubstantial, and yet properly functioning
nature of all things and processes. Persons who are so
blind live within complex sets of religious or worldly

ideas and emotions that they believe to be final, established, and therefore real.

They project this self-created world onto their
ideas of past and future and the present moment.
They try to crystallize reality into permanent shapes
and categories. In this way they veil the path of insight, the spiritual path which reveals the innate clarity, freedom, and radiant transparency of What Is."

Prajnaparamita

A recluse, Bhaddiya, walked in lonely places and sat
at the foot of great trees. He was often heard to exclaim, "Ah, it's bliss, it's bliss!"

Monks, who were forever hearing this, believed he
must be referring to the wealthy life he had left. They
told the Buddha what they thought. He sent one of
them to fetch Bhaddiya, and when Bhaddiya arrived,
the Buddha asked him:

"You are often heard repeating, 'Ah, it's bliss, it's
bliss!' What is your motive, when you are in the
forests, to exclaim in this way?"

"Formerly, Buddha, when I enjoyed a royal life
within a palace, there were guards set to protect
me—in the district as well as the grounds. But although so guarded and protected, I was fearful, anxious, trembling, and afraid. But now, you see, I live

in the forest by the roots of trees and in lonely places, and although I am alone, I feel there is nothing to fear. So I am confident and unafraid and live easily, unstartled, with a light heart, and feeling naturally at home like some wild animal. That was my motive for exclaiming 'Ah, it's bliss, it's bliss!'"

The Buddha honored him with a verse:

For the one who has no inner, angry thoughts,
Who has gone past being a someone, a this or a
   that,
That one is free from fear and is blissful.
Even the gods cannot win such serenity.

Udana Sutta

The Buddha was teaching his followers in the Bamboo Grove by the Squirrels' Feeding Ground near the town of Rajgir. A leper who lived by begging in the town came across the throng listening to the Buddha and at the sight of so many people hoped there might be an almsgiving of food. But as he drew nearer, he thought, No, there's no food here. This is the Buddha giving his teaching. I might as well listen.

The Buddha was wondering, among all these people, who was capable of understanding the teaching. He caught sight of the leper, who was sitting apart from the crowd, and thought—With his misfortunes, he will understand. So he talked of almsgiving and generosity, of the dangers of clinging to a sensual life, and of how blissful was freedom from the dictates of the self. He saw the leper's face become softened and elated and so he talked about the truths that the awakened discover for themselves—the ways conditioned life arises and the breaking of bonds into the unconditioned.

As a white cloth free from stains is ready for the dye, so within the leper's mind arose the pure and stainless understanding of the unconditioned and the timeless. He saw that what is born must die but that which is unborn is undying. He saw the truth, reached the truth, understood the truth, plunged into the truth, crossed over beyond doubting, was free from all questions, and with total confidence rose from his seat and made his way through the crowd to the Buddha. He exclaimed:"It is wonderful! It is just as though you have lifted up the fallen, discovered the hidden, pointed out the way to the confused, shown light in the darkness. May you accept me as a follower, as one who from now to the end of my life will take refuge in the truth."

The Buddha said: "You are one who is ready to take the teachings and to outshine many with your beauty."

Udana Sutta

The Buddha was staying near Kosambi. The monks of Kosambi were forever disputing with each other, quarreling and wounding each other with harsh words. One came to the Buddha and told him of the situation, adding: "It would be good if, out of compassion, you were to approach these monks."

The Buddha went to the monks and said. "Enough, monks. No more disputes, quarrels, contention, or argument."

But when he left they started again. "Please come back and stay for a bit," he was asked, "You are untroubled and will bring ease to the situation."

So he went back a second time, and yet again a third. After the third time, he rose early in the morning, took his bowl and robe, and went to Kosambi for food. When his meal was over, he went back to the monks and said:

"None of you feels a fool when you all bawl at each other in chorus. Nor, though you are dividing the order, does anyone think anything of it. With wandering wits, you range all over the field of speculation, not even knowing where you are going or what is leading you on. If you keep thinking 'That man has abused me,' holding it as a much-cherished grievance, your anger will never be allayed. If you can put down that fury-inducing thought, your anger will lessen. Fury will never end fury, it will just ricochet on and on. Only putting it down will end such an abysmal state. Even villains who maim and kill and steal can know a companionship together—why should it not be possible for you?

"Find a friend to be with and stay in that relationship, avoiding the dangers of hurting others. Stay with your friend and become mindful and joyful. If you can find no friend, then go on by yourself. Better to carry on alone than live with the foolish. Journey on alone, unconcerned, working no evil, like the bull elephant in the elephant jungle."

Sunnata Vagga

The Buddha told a story to his monks:

"A young widower was devoted to his little son. But while he was away on business, the whole village was burned to the ground by bandits, who took away the little boy. When the father returned and found only ruins, he was brokenhearted. He thought that the charred remains of an infant was his own child, so he organized a cremation, collected the ashes, and carried them always in a special bag.

"One day his real son managed to escape from the bandits and found his way back to his old home. His father had rebuilt the house. When he arrived, late one night, and knocked on the door, his father called, 'Who is there?'

"'It is I, your son. Please let me in.'

"The father, still carrying the ashes and hopelessly sad, thought this must be some wretched boy making fun of him and he shouted, 'Go away!'

"The boy knocked and called again and again, but the father always made the same response, and at last the boy left, never to come back again."

When he had told this story, the Buddha added, "If you cling to an idea as the unalterable truth, then when the truth does come in person and knock at your door, you will not be able to open the door and accept it."

Udana Sutta

O monks, even if you have insight that is pure and clear but you cling to it, fondle it and treasure it, depend on it and are attached to it, then you do not understand that the teaching is like a raft that carries you across the water to the farther shore but is then to be put down and not clung to.

Majjhima Nikaya

There are people who suffer but do not understand why. They don't know how the suffering arose or when it will end or how to get to that end.

They have not understood that grasping is one

of the causes of suffering. People grasp at circumstances, they attach themselves. But often this results in a new misery. They grasp things out of ignorance because they are confused and muddled, and thus they wander endlessly on. If they could stop acting on impulse, could walk toward knowledge, and could let go of grasping, they would not go on suffering.

Contact, the point where the senses meet the object, is enthralling for some people. It is so exciting and gripping that they are washed by tides of desire and drift along a pointless road. But whether sensation is pleasant or unpleasant or merely neutral, it should always be remembered that it's a fragile experience and one should see its beginning and end. That is the way to help one to loosen one's grasp.

All the delightful things of the world—sweet sounds, lovely forms, all the pleasant tastes and touches and thoughts—these are all agreed to bring happiness if they are not grasped and possessed.

But if you regard them merely as pleasures for your own use and satisfaction and do not see them as passing wonders, they will bring suffering.

Be aware of this paradox, for if you are blind to the way things are you will not be able to make out anything, even though you might be right on top of it.

The teaching about the way things are is not a way to enlightenment for someone who is still filled with desires or who still longs to be a this or a that. But those who do understand it will become beings of distinction, dispersing all the forces of confusion.

Sutta Nipata

Ajita asked: "What is it that smothers the world and makes it so hard to see? What is it that pollutes the world and seems to threaten it?"

The Buddha answered: "It is ignorance that smothers, and it is carelessness and greed that make it invisible. The hunger of craving pollutes the world, and the pain of suffering causes the greatest fear."

Sutta Nipata

"It seems as though the rivers of craving are running in every direction," said Ajita. "How can we dam them and hold them back? What can we use to close the floodgates?"

The Buddha said: "Any river can be stopped with the dam of mindfulness. Caring and thoughtfulness are the flood stoppers. With wisdom you can close the floodgate."

Sutta Nipata

If any recluses or followers do not understand objectively that the enjoyment of sense pleasures is enjoyment, that the unsatisfactoriness of their passing is unsatisfactoriness, and that liberation from their tyranny is liberation—then it's not possible that they will properly understand what the desire for sense pleasures is or that they will be able to bring anyone else to understand it. But if they do understand objectively the arising and ceasing of sense pleasures, their frequent unsatisfactoriness, and the way to freedom from attachment to them, they will be able to instruct other people to that end.

Majjhima Nikaya

You should inquire deeply and directly into the distress of the mind and find out what has been created and who is the self that is suffering. Without this understanding, you can't develop clarity and the ability to help others. A person may be expert at undoing knots, but if he never sees that there is a knot in front of him, how will he undo it? Without clear and direct looking, you will be locked into time and space and unable to free yourself from the material world.

Surangama Sutra

 TRUTH

The Kalamas of Kesaputta came to the Buddha and said:

"There are some monks and teachers who come to Kesaputta. They talk a lot about their own ideas but they despise and take to pieces the views of others. And as we listen to them, we can't help feeling some doubt. We waver between who is telling the truth and who is telling lies."

"It's a good thing that you do have doubt, Kalamas. You may well waver, for your wavering is all to do with a matter that is wide open to doubt.

"So listen to me, Kalamas. Don't go by gossip and rumor, nor by what's told you by others, nor by what you hear said, nor even by the authority of your traditional teachings. Don't go by reasoning, nor by inferring one thing from another, nor by argument about methods, nor from liking an opinion, nor from awe of the teacher and thinking he must be deferred to.

"Instead, Kalamas, when you know from within yourselves that certain teachings are not good, that when put into practice they lead to loss and suffering, you must then trust yourselves and reject them."

Anguttara Nikaya

Sakka asked the Buddha:

"Do different religious teachers head for the same goal or practice the same disciplines or aspire to the same thing?"

"No, Sakka, they do not. And why? This world is made up of myriad different states of being, and people adhere to one or another of these states and become tenaciously possessive of them, saying, 'This alone is true, everything else is false.' It is like a territory that they believe is theirs. So all religious teachers do not teach the same goal or the same discipline, nor do they aspire to the same thing.

"But if you find truth in any religion or philosophy, then accept that truth without prejudice."

Digha Nikaya

A questioner asked the Buddha:

"Life seems a tangle—
An inner tangle and an outer tangle.
This generation is hopelessly tangled up.

And so I ask the Buddha this question:
Who will succeed in disentangling this tangle?"

The Buddha replied:

"When a wise one, thoughtful and good,
Develops a greater consciousness,
He will understand the tangle.
As a truth follower, ardent and wise,
He will succeed in disentangling the tangle."

Samyutta Nikaya

The truth is noble and sweet; the truth can free you from all ills. There is no savior in the world like the truth.

Have confidence in the truth, even though you may not be able to understand it, even though its sweetness has a bitter edge, even though at first you may shrink from it. Trust in the truth.

The truth is best as it is. No one can alter it, neither can anyone improve it. Have faith in the truth and live it.

The self is in a fever; the self is forever changing, like a dream. But the truth is whole, sublime and everlasting. Nothing is immortal except the truth, for truth alone exists forever.

Majjhima Nikaya

From time to time there appears in this world one who has seen the truth, a fully awakened one, blessed by the truth, abounding in happiness, a teacher of wisdom and goodness, a buddha. He, by himself, thoroughly knows and sees this universe, and knowing it, he makes his knowledge known to others. The truth, lovely in its origin, lovely in its progress, lovely in its consummation, he proclaims. A new life he makes known, in all its fullness.

Tevigga Sutta

When he was dying, the Buddha said to his followers:

"Hold fast to the truth as a lamp that shines in the darkness. Seek salvation in the truth alone.

"Those who either now or after I am dead hold fast to the truth as their lamp and do not look for light from anywhere else—it is they who will reach nirvana."

Majjhima Nikaya

Those who argue and discuss without understanding the truth are lost amid all the forms of relative knowledge, running about here and there and trying to justify their view of the substance of ego.

If you realize the self in your inmost consciousness,

it will appear in its purity. This is the womb of wonder, which is not the realm of those who live only by reason.

Pure in its own nature and free from the categories of finite and infinite, Universal Mind is the undefiled wonder, which is wrongly apprehended by many.

Lankavatara Sutra

The truth indeed has never been preached by the Buddha, seeing that one has to realize it within oneself.

Lamkara Sutra

The one who has entered a solitary place,
Whose mind is calm and who sees the way,
To that one comes insight and truth
And rapturous joy transcending any other.

Dhammapada

A brahman was making a ritual fire for worship. The Buddha said to him:

"You should not imagine, brahman, that insight comes by merely laying sticks on a fire. You should trust to the truth that is within you to enrich your spiritual life and not to external rituals. Having departed from that way of doing things altogether, I kindle my fire within. Here the controlled tongue is the sacrificial spoon and the heart is the altar of the fire."

Samyutta Nikaya

Never think that I believe I should set out a "system of teaching" to help people understand the way. Never cherish such a thought. What I proclaim is the truth as I have discovered it and "a system of teaching" has no meaning because the truth can't be cut up into pieces and arranged in a system.

Diamond Sutra

One of his followers urged the Buddha to perform a miracle in order to attract some nonbelievers. The Buddha replied:

"I detest and will not undertake the so-called miracles of magic power and divination. I and my followers attract nonbelievers only by the miracle of truth."

Digha Nikaya

Just as the word *chariot* is merely a means of expressing how axle, body, wheel, and poles are brought together in a certain relationship, but when we look at each of them one by one there is no chariot in an absolute sense; and just as the word *house* is a way of expressing how wood and other materials stand in relationship to each other in a certain space, but in the absolute sense there is no house; and just as the word *fist* is an expression for the fingers and thumb in relationship, and *tree* for trunk, branches, leaves, and so on, but in an absolute sense there is no fist or tree—in exactly the same way the words *living entity* and *person* are but ways of expressing the relationship of body, feeling, and consciousness, but when we come to examine the elements of being, one by one, we find there is no entity there. In the absolute sense there is only name and form and the mystery which they express. Such ideas as "I" and "I am" are not absolute.

Visuddhi Magga

Accept my words only when you have examined them for yourselves; do not accept them simply because of the reverence you have for me. Those who only have faith in me and affection for me will not find the final freedom. But those who have faith in the truth and are determined on the path, they will find awakening.

Majjhima Nikaya

"Monks, if people speak badly of me or badly of the teaching or of our order of monks, you should not because of their ill will hold any thoughts of enmity toward them or any spite, nor even be at all worried. For if you are angry or displeased with them it will hurt you more than them. Indeed, if you were to feel angry or displeased, would you then be able to know what is well intended and what is badly intended from others?"

"No, we would not be able to know this."

"So, if others speak ill of me or the teaching or the order, you should with goodwill unravel the untruth of what they have said and make it all clear to them, saying, 'For this reason, that is false; for this reason, that is untrue; these things are not within us.'"

Digha Nikaya

Of all the medicines in the world
Myriad and various
There is none like the medicine of Truth
Therefore, O followers, drink of this

Dhammapada

Few cross the river to the farther shore. The rest run up and down this side of the torrent.

But those who pursue the truth will reach the farther shore, and pass through the realm of death, which is so hard to cross.

Leaving the way of darkness, the wise man will follow the way of light. Giving up his security, he will enter into inner solitude, knowing the road to be hard.

Putting away craving and freeing himself from possessions, the wise man will rid himself of all dark thoughts.

With his mind full of regard for the truth, with energy, concentration, and calmness, clinging to nothing and overcoming all dark thoughts, he is awakened and enters nirvana in this world.

Dhammapada

It is good to control your words and thoughts. The seeker who is in control feels free and joyful. Listen to that seeker who guards his tongue and speaks wisely. Such a one is humble and does not exalt himself. He follows the universal Law in his daily life. When you are master of your concentration, you will delight in inner solitude and meditation.

The seeker who loves the truth and always reflects upon it will always be sustained by it.

Empty your boat, seeker, and you will travel more

swiftly. Lighten the load of craving and opinions and you will reach nirvana sooner.

Dhammapada

Anyone who, even for a second, feels a pure, clear confidence on hearing the truth will experience immeasurable happiness. Why? Because, at that moment, that person is not caught up in the concept of a self or a living being or a life span. He is not caught up in concepts about the world, nor is he caught up in concepts about nothingness. He does not take any notice of the idea that this or that is a sign, or this or that is not a sign.

For if you are caught up in ideas, then you will be caught up in the self. And even if you are caught up in ideas about nothingness, you will still be caught up in the self. That's why we should not get attached to the belief that things either exist or do not exist. This is the hidden meaning when I say that my teachings are a raft to be abandoned when you see true being.

Diamond Sutra

Monks, this committed life is not lived in order to deceive people, or to convert them. It is not lived for the sake of gain or honor or reputation or financial profit. There is no idea of "let me draw people's attention to me by being a this or a that." No, monks, this committed life is lived for the sake of seeing into things and understanding them.

Itivuttaka Sutta

An inquirer asked the Buddha: "People are fixed in their pet beliefs. They wrangle with each other, saying, 'Hold this truth and you are saved; reject it and you are lost.' In this way they argue and call each other fools. Which way is right, when they all pose as experts?"

The Buddha answered, "Well, if dissent denotes a fool, then they are all fools, since each has his own view. I do not call anything true if it involves calling another person a fool, because that means possessing a 'truth' as one's own."

"But what makes these 'experts' preach their opinion and call it truth?" asked the inquirer. "Is it an inheritance of humankind to do this, or is it merely something they gain satisfaction from?"

"Apart from consciousness," answered the Buddha, "no absolute truths exist. False reasoning declares one view to be true and another view wrong. It is delight in their dearly held opinions that makes them assert that anyone who disagrees is bound to come to a bad end. But no true seeker becomes embroiled in all this. Pass by peacefully and go a stainless way, free from theories, lusts, and dogmas."

Majjhima Nikaya

The wanderer Bhaggava accused the Buddha of saying that the universe was caused merely by chance. The Buddha replied:

"I have heard others of your sect, Bhaggava, say that when I awoke and found the truth, which was beautiful, I remained in that bliss and then regarded the universe as ugly and meaningless in comparison.

"But I never taught that, Bhaggava. This is what I do say: 'Whenever one awakes and finds the beautiful, then one knows indeed what beauty is.'"

Majjhima Nikaya

Subhuti asked: "You say, Honored One, that a follower of the way does not need to build up goodness and happiness. Why is that?"

The Buddha replied: "Subhuti, a true follower will express goodness and happiness but will not be caught up in the concepts of goodness and happiness. That's why I say that he does not need to build up

goodness and happiness, which would only be concept traps, for goodness and happiness will be there
without any idea of them."

Diamond Sutra

 LIFE AND DEATH

A wandering monk called Vaccha asked the Buddha
if the Buddha would still exist after death. The Buddha replied:

"Vaccha, the idea that I would exist or not exist after death—such ideas lead to dense jungles and arid
deserts, to entanglements as though caught by thorns.
They bring about anger, delusion, and argument and
they do not bring about peace, knowledge, or wisdom leading to enlightenment. I do not take up any
of these ideas."

"Then has the Buddha any belief of his own?"

"Vaccha, I have nothing to do with beliefs or theories, but declare what I know. I declare the nature
of form, how it arises and how it perishes; the nature
of perception, how it arises and how it perishes.
And because I have completely abandoned all fan-
tasies, false ideas, and imaginings about the nature
of self or anything to do with the self, I am freed
from self."

"But," asked Vaccha persistently, "when one who has attained this emancipation of mind dies, where does he go, where is he reborn?"

"The word *reborn* does not fit the case."

"Then is he not reborn?"

"To say that he is not reborn does not fit the case either. Nor should you say that he is both reborn and not reborn or, indeed, that he is neither reborn nor not reborn."

"I am totally bewildered, Buddha, and my faith in you has gone."

"Never mind being bewildered. This is a deep and difficult doctrine to understand. Imagine there is a fire in front of you. You see it burning and know that it can only burn if it has fuel. And then you see that it has gone out. Now, somebody asks you, to which quarter has the fire gone—east, west, north, or south? What do you say?"

"I would say that such a question does not fit the case, Buddha. For the fire depends on fuel, and when there is no more fuel, the fire is said to be out through lack of nourishment."

"In just the same way, Vaccha, the body in which one can see the truth will die out, like a fan palm, without any future. But that which is the truth, that which is existence itself, is there although it is deep and infinitely hard to understand. Like the great ocean, one cannot fathom it. And so it does not fit the case to say that I will be reborn or will not be reborn."

Digha Nikaya

Attentiveness is the path to true life;
Indifference is the path to death.
The attentive do not die;
The indifferent are as if they are dead already.

Dhammapada

One day Malunkyaputta came to the Buddha and said, "You have not told us whether the world is eternal or not, whether the soul is the same as the body, or whether the self exists after death. If you can explain these things, I will continue to be a monk, otherwise I shall leave."

The Buddha replied: "Did I promise all these explanations when you first joined us? Or did you stipulate you must know them?"

"No," Malunkyaputta confessed.

"Then listen to me. Suppose a man were wounded by an arrow and when the surgeon arrived, he said to him, 'Don't pull out this arrow until I know who shot it, what tree it comes from, who made it, and what kind of bow was used.' Certainly the man would die before he discovered the answers. In the same way, if you say you will not be a monk unless I solve all the questions of the world, you are likely to die unsatisfied.

"To be a follower of the truth does not depend on any such answers. Whether the world is eternal or transient, there is suffering, and I teach the way to understand it. My teaching does not depend on whether I exist after death or not, because I am concerned with suffering here and now. To all of you I have explained what should be explained and not explained that which is not relevant to the end of suffering and finding of happiness."

Majjhima Nikaya

Once, two very old brahmans, both 120 years old, came to see the Buddha. They sat down before him and said:

"We are brahmans, frail and old. We have not done anything noble or even particularly worthwhile. So now there is nothing to reduce our fear of death. Please show us a way to happiness."

The Buddha said: "Yes, brahmans, you are truly frail and old and now you are full of fear. This world is flooded with old age, sickness, and death. But if you can practice some insight into your deeds, some control over your words, and some contemplation of your thoughts, that will provide you with a refuge and a shelter.

"Your life is nearly over. No one is immune from old age and death. Remembering death and keeping it in your mind, practice performing good deeds that lead to happiness for others. One who performs good deeds and is thoughtful will become harmonious in body, speech, and mind. He will find that death is not to be feared but indeed brings happiness."

Anguttara Nikaya

Whether good sages appear or not, there is an established condition of life and that is that all phenomena have causes, are born, and will die. All conditioned things are impermanent. And whether a wise one appears or not, this established law of life causes suffering and grief. And whether there is an awakened one or not, a third condition of life is that there is no permanent self. The one who has awakened fully understands this. That one will declare, "All conditioned things are not self."

Anguttara Nikaya

Kutadanta accused the Buddha: "I am told that you teach the law of life and the way, yet you tear down religion. Your followers despise rituals and abandon sacrifices. But reverence for the gods can only be shown through sacrifices. The very nature of religion is that of worship and sacrifice."

The Buddha replied: "Greater than the massacring of bullocks is the sacrifice of self. He who offers up his evil desires will see the uselessness of slaughtering animals at the altar. Blood has no power to cleanse, but the giving up of harmful actions will make the heart whole. Better than worshipping gods is following the ways of goodness."

Digha Nikaya

Moghavagan came to the Buddha. "I have come to you with a question, great sage. I am afraid of death. Is there any way to look upon the world so as not to be seen by the king of death?"

"Look upon the world as empty," the Buddha replied. "This is the way to overcome death. Cease thinking of yourself as an entity that really exists. If you look on the world in this way, you will never be seen by the king of death."

Sutta Nipata

A recluse, renowned as an enlightened man, came to a heartfelt decision that he was not in fact fully liberated. He thought the Buddha's teaching would help him and he traveled across central India until he reached the city of Savatthi, where the Buddha was staying. He went to the Buddha's meditation center and asked to see the Buddha.

"He is out on his begging round," he was told. "Wait here and rest from your journey and you will see him soon."

"I can't wait," answered the recluse. "Show me the way and I will find him."

He set off again and came to the city center. There he saw the Buddha, surrounded by an atmosphere of peace and harmony and going with his begging bowl from house to house. The recluse fell to his knees and embraced the Buddha's feet.

"You are fully liberated," he said to the Buddha. "Please teach me a practice that will bring liberation for me."

"Gladly," said the Buddha, "but not here, this is not the time or place. Go to my meditation center and wait for me."

"No, I can't wait."

"Not even for a short time?"

"No, for even in such a short time I might die or

you might die. Now, sir, this is the time. Please teach me now."

The Buddha looked at him and saw that death was near. He realized that the teaching must be given at once. But what to teach while standing in the middle of the road? He decided to put the essential teaching in just a few words.

"In your seeing," he said, "there should be only the seeing. In your hearing, nothing but the hearing; in your smelling, tasting, and touching, nothing but smelling, tasting, and touching; in your thinking, nothing but the thought."

The recluse was of such pure mind that these words told him all he needed. No judgments, no evaluations, a freeing of the mind from all its conditioning by a simple experience of things just as they are. He sat down in the road there and then to fix his attention on clarity, and when death came he had found liberation.

Khuddaka Nikaya

The Buddha was warned that a robber and murderer named Angulimala inhabited a stretch of country he wanted to cross. So fierce and destructive was Angulimala that only large parties of people would walk over this land together. His habit was to take a finger from each of his victims and wear it round his neck, giving him the nickname Necklace of Fingers.

Unperturbed by these reports, the Buddha set out across this land on his own. Angulimala saw him coming and was astonished that there was nobody with him. He determined to kill him and, armed with his sword, came up behind the Buddha. But strangely he found that although the Buddha was walking at an ordinary pace, he seemed unable to catch up with him.

"Stand still, recluse!" he shouted.

"I am standing still, Angulimala. You, too, stand still."

Angulimala thought, These holy men are supposed to tell the truth, yet this one, while he is walking, says he is standing still.

"You tell me to stand still, but I am not walking," he shouted, "whereas you who are walking say you are still. How is it that *you* are standing still but *I* am not?"

The Buddha turned round. "My legs move but my mind is still," he said. "Your legs are still but your mind moves all the time in a fire of anger, hatred, and feverish desire. Therefore, I am still but you are not."

Angulimala was struck by the truth of this. He thought, It's a long time since I paid any attention to a sage, but this recluse has penetrated my whole nature. I will take up his teaching and lose my feverish mind.

He threw his sword into a pit and knelt down by the Buddha's feet. "Please liberate me," he asked.

The Buddha looked at him with compassion. "Come, monk," he said, by that word giving him the status he asked for, and the two went on together.

Majjhima Nikaya

All tremble when there is a weapon,
Everyone fears death;
Feeling for others as for oneself,
One should neither kill nor cause to kill.

Dhammapada

If there were no freedom, beings could never disentangle themselves from the world. But since there is freedom to transcend the world, beings are able to become disentangled.

Anguttara Nikaya

While the Buddha was in the town of Shravasti, he called the monks to him and said, "I will teach you what is meant by knowing the best way to live independently."

"We are listening," the monks told him.
He said:

Do not go after the past,
Nor lose yourself in the future.
For the past no longer exists,
And the future is not yet here.
By looking deeply at things just as they are,
In this moment, here and now,
The seeker lives calmly and freely.
You should be attentive today,
For waiting until tomorrow is too late.
Death can come and take us by surprise--
How can we gainsay it?
The one who knows
How to live attentively
Night and day
Is the one who knows
The best way to be independent.

Bhaddekaratta Sutra

TIME AND INFINITY

If the element of the truth seeker did not exist in
    everyone,
There would be no turning away from craving,
Nor could there be a longing for nirvana,
Nor a seeking for it, nor a resolve to find it.

Visuddhi Magga

There is a sphere where there is neither earth nor
water nor heat nor air, for it is beyond the field of
matter; nor is it the sphere of infinite space, or consciousness, for it is beyond the field of mind. There is
not the condition of nothingness, neither is there the
state of this world or another world, nor sun nor
moon. This is the uncreated.

This condition I call neither arising nor passing
away, neither dying nor being born. It is without form
and without change. It is the eternal, which never

originates and never passes away. To find it is the end of sorrow.

There *is* this unborn, uncreated, unformed, and unconditioned. Were there not this unborn, uncreated, unformed, and unconditioned, there would be no transcendence from the world of the born, created, formed, and conditioned.

But since, monks, there is the unborn, uncreated, unformed, and unconditioned, therefore there can be transcendence for the born, created, formed, and conditioned.

Udana Sutta

The Buddha was asked: "Is there only one summit of consciousness or are there several?"

He replied: "One and several. As one state of consciousness is realized, then the next is seen. Thus there are several and there is one."

He was then asked: "Which is first, awareness or knowledge?"

"Awareness arises first and then comes knowledge. One can then say, 'Because of my awareness, I know this as a fact.'"

Digha Nikaya

What are the results of a person's past life? We can
never know them by thinking or guessing and so we
should not speculate about them. To try to find them
out is to bring distress and distraction. Do not set
yourself up as a judge of others or make assumptions
about their motives. You can destroy yourself by
holding judgments about others.

Anguttara Nikaya

It is through not understanding, not penetrating four
things that we have run so erratically, wandered on so
long in this round of existence, both you and I. What
are the four? Goodness, concentration, wisdom, and
liberation. When these four things are understood
and penetrated, craving for superficial existence is
rooted out and that which leads to continued return
to the same conditions is ended. There is no more
constant journeying.

Digha Nikaya

Suppose a goldsmith takes his tongs and puts some
gold into the furnace to melt it. If he blows on the
heat too much, it will get too hot, but if he sprinkles
too much water, it will cool down. If he constantly

takes it out and looks at it, it will not reach refinement. But if he does all these things from time to time, aware of the nature of gold, it will become easily molded and bright.

In the same way, there are three qualities that a practitioner should pay attention to — concentration, determination, and equanimity. If he pays the right attention to these at the right time, then his mind will become like gold, pliant and brilliant and pure.

Anguttara Nikaya

Where is thought? It can never be seen or even apprehended. It is like a magical illusion, for with imagination it colors the world. Searching for thought and unable to see it, a person looks for its origin. And it seems to be that where there is an object thought arises. Thought does not arise without an object. Can thought look at thought? No. Just as the blade of a sword cannot cut itself, or a fingertip touch itself, so thought cannot see thought.

Sikshasamuccaya

When the perfect wisdom is first seen, a new perception comes into being that does not depend on any structure. The great quest of the seeker now blossoms as various vast and mysterious doors swing open at the mere touch of the new perception.

There is the door that opens to a vista of the essenceless essence, that which is the real nature of the manifested world. There is the door of liberation from a merely partial perception or muddled perspective of this real nature. And there is the door that opens directly into the authentic realization of this true nature.

There is the wonderful door that opens into an intensity of sights and sounds, color and beauty. And there is the door of balance and ease through which one looks in awe at all the limitless structures of the world as one looks at the star-studded night sky. And there is the door to the exquisite happiness that would never want to own any worldly treasures or to possess even that same happiness. finally, there is the door of total awakening itself.

Prajnaparamita

There are three ways of seeing life. In one people stick fast. In another they go to excess. In the third they see correctly.

In the first way, people take pleasure in all the things of life—in possessions and happenings, in families and continuation. When a teaching is proclaimed that advises nonattachment and going beyond the dictates of the self, their heart does not leap up and they are not drawn to it.

In the second way, people are afflicted by hatred of life. Just as attached to life, they nonetheless revile it and make a bad thing of it to excess.

In the third way, people see life as it is—forever being and ceasing to be. They accept it willingly but are not attached and do not despair. It is they who begin to know the unconditioned.

> The one who beholds that which has become as
>   become
> Passes beyond that becoming
> And is released from craving for sensation.
> In that which really is, he understands becoming.
> Free from longing for birth or death,
> He finds the true meaning of the end of
>   becoming.
>
> *Itivuttaka Sutta*

If you seek after truth, you should investigate things in such a way that your consciousness as you investigate is not distracted by what you find, or diffused and scattered; neither is it fixed and set. For the one

who is not swayed, there will be a transcending of
birth, death, and time.

> Whether you walk or stand or lie down,
> Stretch your limbs or draw them in again,
> Let you do all these things attentively,
> Above, across, and back again.
> Whatever your place in the world,
> Let you be the one who views the movement
> Of all compounded things with attention.
>
> *Itivuttaka Sutta*

If you want to know the past, to know what has
caused you, look at yourself in the present, for that is
the past's effect. If you want to know your future,
then look at yourself in the present, for that is the
cause of the future.

> *Majjhima Nikaya*

Subhuti, how does a person first feel a need to save beings? He becomes aware of that kind of wise insight
which shows him beings as on their way to destroying
themselves. Great compassion then takes hold of him.
He surveys the world, and what he sees fills him with
agitation. So many carry the burden of actions that

will bring their own punishment in their wake; others have been born in unfortunate circumstances in which they know nothing of the truth; and yet others are doomed to be killed in wars or to be enveloped in a net of false views or to fail to find the way; and there are yet others who have had a fortunate birth and who have begun to find freedom but have lost it again.

So such a person radiates great friendliness and compassion over all these beings and gives his attention to them, thinking, "I would like to save these beings, I would like to release them from all their sufferings." But he does not make this desire into an attachment, for he never turns his back on full enlightenment. For he knows that only when his thoughts are supported by perfect wisdom will they bear fruit. Only from the realm of perfect wisdom can he point out the path, shed light in darkness, set people free, and cleanse the organs of vision of all beings.

Prajnaparamita

If anyone says that a person *must* reap according to his deeds, if anyone thinks the law of karma is inexorable, then he is saying that there is no spiritual life or growth and nor is there any opportunity to bring confusion to an end. But if anyone says that what a person reaps is *in accordance* with his deeds, in that case a spiritual life can exist and there is opportunity for realization.

Anguttara Nikaya

You cannot expect to have the conditioned without the unconditioned. The conditioned world cannot exist without nirvana. Nor can you expect to have the unconditioned without the conditioned—you cannot have nirvana apart from the world. Their sameness is the truth of reality. The wise person lives this truth and at the same time engages in good works. Without ever swerving from the realization of the truth that all things are empty of entity or self, he inspires all creatures to free themselves from the idea of self. Emptiness means empty of all notions and assumptions. When empty of all assumptions, the world is like a magical creation; the body is a wonder, and wisdom is a wonder. They are magical by coming into existence and passing away. Anything that has a beginning and an end in time is illusory and magical. Only nirvana has no beginning and no end and is by its nature reality, undeluded, beyond illusion.

Subhuti asked: "How should an ordinary person be taught this truth?"

The Buddha answered: "By asking the person this: 'How can that which existed in the past become nonexistent now?' This inquiry will lead to the realization that there is nothing that ever existed that is a permanent entity or an eternal self. Then the questioner will see that there is both existence and nonexistence."

Prajnaparamita

It is a defect in language that words suggest permanent realities and people do not see through this deception. But mere words cannot create reality. Thus people speak of a final goal and believe it is real, but it is a form of words and the goal as such is without substance. The one who realizes the emptiness of objects and concepts does not depend on words. Perfect wisdom is beyond definition, and pathlessness is the way to it.

The wise one treads this path for the direct realization of impermanence and for the direct realization of understanding. This, then, is perfect wisdom. Such a one should tread this path knowing that attachment and attractions are neither good nor harmful, even enlightenment is neither good nor harmful, because perfect wisdom is not meant to promote good or harm for that person. However, even though there is no intention of good or harm, it does confer endless blessing.

Prajnaparamita

Sakka asked: "What is the cause of self-interest?"

The Buddha answered: "It is perception of the world as one's object."

"How does one overcome this perception of the world as apart from oneself?"

"By acting for the increase of goodness and happiness. It is in this way that the world ceases to be one's object."

Digha Nikaya

There is a way of skillful means that is called "like the sun." Just as the sun ripens the growing plant, so a skillful person, like the sun, can mature the seed of enlightenment in others. Then, too, as the sun never stops giving out heat, so the skill of this person establishes all beings in compassion. Third, as the sun melts frozen things, so a skillful person seeing, as it were, the antidotes, melts away cravings and obsessions. As the sun takes away the darkness, so this person—recognizing all that is there in the other—takes away the darkness of ignorance. And as the sun warms everything up equally, so the skillful one gladdens all beings, for the means he uses are like the warmth and radiance of the sun.

Prajnaparamita

When people have come to know fully the satisfactions that the world can give, also the misery that can be caused—when they understand that there can be freedom from both desire and sorrow—then they are released from the shackles of the world, from its confines and limitations. They live with a liberated heart. They come to know the real meaning of the world, the way things arise and cease and the consciousness that transcends both the arising and the ceasing.

Anguttara Nikaya

WISDOM

All that we are is the result of our thoughts; it is founded on our thoughts and made up of our thoughts. With our thoughts we make the world. If you speak or act with a harmful thought, trouble will follow you as the wheel follows the ox that draws the cart.

All that we are is the result of our thoughts; it is founded on our thoughts and made up of our thoughts. With our thoughts we make the world. If you speak or act with a harmonious thought, happiness will follow you as your own shadow, never leaving you.

Dhammapada

Suppose a person is in need of sound timber and he searches for it. He comes across a great, upstanding tree—all good wood—but he ignores the trunk and takes the easier branches and bark instead, hoping that this is good timber. A wiser person would at once say, "That one surely can't tell the difference between sound timber and bark. He has nothing there that will serve his needs."

In the same way, the essence of the dedicated life does not consist of quick gains, honor, and good name, nor in the profit that comes from observing moral rules. Nor yet even in knowledge or insight. The real heart's release—the trunk of the tree—that heart's release is the meaning, the essence, the goal of living the dedicated life.

Majjhima Nikaya

A monk can be very gentle, very peaceful, while there are no hard words to assail him. But when hard words are directed at him, it is then that he must be really gentle and peaceful.

Majjhima Nikaya

Two things will lead you to supreme understanding. What are those two? Tranquillity and insight.

If you develop tranquillity, what benefit can you expect? Your mind will develop. The benefit of a developed mind is that you are no longer a slave to your impulses.

If you develop insight, what benefit will it bring? You will find wisdom. And the point of developing wisdom is that it brings you freedom from the blindness of ignorance.

A mind held bound by unconsidered impulse and ignorance can never develop true understanding. But by way of tranquillity and insight the mind will find freedom.

Anguttara Nikaya

Before teaching others, you have to know what you are teaching thoroughly. So it's very important for you yourself to practice continually. Without having yourself experienced what you are teaching, you cannot properly teach others. One who is sunk in the mud is unable to pull out another sunk in the mud.

Majjhima Nikaya

A brahman said to the Buddha: "For my part, I say this, this is my view. If I speak of what I've seen or heard or sensed, there is no harm resulting from that."

The Buddha replied: "For my part, brahman, I do not say that everything one has seen, heard, or sensed should be said or should not be said. It's a question of timing. One should be aware of what is the right time and what is the wrong time. It's possible to speak openly and be misunderstood. But if open speaking is at the right time and the right occasion, then you should do it."

Anguttara Nikaya

Monks, the lion, king of beasts, comes forth from his lair in the evening. He stretches himself and surveys all the four directions. Having done this, he utters his great lion's roar three times. Then he sets off in search of prey.

When the animals hear the sound of the roar, they tremble and quake. Those that live in holes dive into them. Water dwellers hurry to the water. The forest creatures hide within the trees. The birds fly up to the top branches.

In the villages, the elephants pull and tear at their leather straps until they break them. Then they run to and fro in a panic, letting their excrement pour out. For such is the power of the lion, king of beasts, mighty and majestic.

In the same way, monks, when a sage arises in the world, one who is enlightened, perfect in wisdom and conduct, a knower of all the worlds and a teacher of all those who can be taught, teaching: "This is the self; this is the origin of the self; this is the liberation of the self; this is the way leading to that liberation"—then, monks, whatever gods there are, living in their heavenly mansions, on hearing this teaching they fall afraid, quaking and trembling, as if hearing a lion's roar.

"It seems that although we thought ourselves permanent, we are not. Although we thought ourselves settled, we are not. Although we thought we would last forever, we will not. So it seems we are impermanent, unsettled, not lasting, and full of self."

This, monks, is how potent and enlightened such a one can be in the world of humans and gods. It is for you to become this.

Anguttara Nikaya

When all the myriad streams that flow in different places, each with its own color and taste, enter the great ocean, they blend and become just one taste, with one name. In the same way, stupidity and wisdom both become one in the awakened mind. When one first starts along the path, there seems to be a distinction that this is stupidity and that is wisdom. But later, when one penetrates more deeply, one finds there is no difference between stupidity and wisdom.

Visuddhi Magga

People lose their wisdom eye through ignorance, doubt, and false ideas. But when they realize the nature of reality, the wisdom eye shines clearly once again. Ordinary people see only through the bodily senses. Thus they see things as though each object had its own ultimate nature and were different from the rest, and it is to this belief they cling. But when they find the wisdom eye of clarity, they realize that all entities are not ultimately real but that nirvana is the true reality.

Surangama Sutra

Subhuti asked: "If all thoughts and emotions are really empty of what we call self, how does a disciple work without a self, how does he become freed?"

The Buddha answered: "If the disciple is aware that the beingness within all beings is not what we call an actual self, that such a conditioned construct as a self has no eternal reality but that the truth is simply the beingness of beings—then he does not lose his foothold in the realm of sanity and wisdom."

Prajnaparamita

Sakuladayi the Wanderer asked the Buddha: "What is the past and what is the future?"

"Let the past be," answered the Buddha, "and forget the future. I will teach you that which is now."

When this condition is, that condition comes
    to be,
With the arising of this, that arises,
When this is not here, that does not come into
    existence,
With the ceasing of this, that too ceases.

                    Majjhima Nikaya

A monk, Meghiya, the Buddha's attendant, was attracted by a beautiful mango grove by a river—a perfect place to meditate, he thought. He asked the Buddha if he might go there. But the Buddha was doubtful.

"Just wait a bit, Meghiya, until some other monk comes along to go with you. We are alone here."

But Meghiya kept on asking, and at last the Buddha replied, "Well, when you talk of striving for concentration, Meghiya, there's really nothing I can say. Do as you want."

So Meghiya went to the mango grove to meditate. But to his astonishment, three disagreeable and wrongful thoughts began to fill his mind—longing for sense pleasures, thoughts of ill will, and a definite wish to harm. "It's strange and amazing," he said to himself, "that after leaving home to be a homeless monk, I am still assailed by these appalling thoughts." He went back to the Buddha and told him what had happened.

"Meghiya, when you are not yet liberated, there are five things you need to help you set your mind free. One is a good friend. Another is practice in upright behavior. Next, you need proper counsel to help you calm your thoughts and enlighten your mind. Fourth, you should make a real effort to get rid of unwholesome mind states. And last, you need the wisdom to see the conditioned rise and fall of events."

Anguttara Sutta

Having tasted the sweetness of inner solitude and calmness, the one who lives by the Law is free from fear and suffering.

It is joy to see such awakened ones, and to live with them is happiness.

To travel with the unawakened makes the journey long and hard and is as painful as traveling with an enemy. But the company of the wise is as pleasant as meeting with friends.

Follow the wise, the intelligent, and the awakened. Follow them as the moon follows the path of the stars.

Dhammapada

Let a person be a light to himself and learn wisdom. When he is free from delusion, he will go beyond birth and death.

No one whose thoughts are only of this world can be a follower of the awakened. All things in this world are changing, but enlightenment remains forever.

Dhammapada

Kutadanta asked: "Where, O Buddha, is nirvana?"

"Nirvana is wherever you live in truth and goodness."

"Then," pursued Kutadanta, "if I understand you correctly, nirvana is not a place. In that case, because it is nowhere, it does not exist."

"You don't understand me," responded the Buddha. "Now listen and answer my questions. Where does the wind dwell?"

"Nowhere."

"Then is there no such thing as the wind?"

Kutadanta made no reply.

"Then where," asked the Buddha, "does wisdom dwell? Is wisdom a locality?"

"Wisdom has no dwelling place."

"So is there then no wisdom, no enlightenment, and no salvation because nirvana is not a locality?"

"I feel, O Buddha, that you're proclaiming a great

doctrine, but I can't grasp it. I seem to get lost. Where, for instance, is the identity of myself? There's a special quality about myself that makes me different from everything else and also from all other selves. And I want that identity, my own self, to continue. So where does that identity dwell?"

"Where indeed?" asked the Buddha. "That self to which you cling is in constant change. Years ago you were a baby, then a youth, and now a man. Which is your true self—that of yesterday, that of today, or that of tomorrow which you so long to preserve?"

"I see I have misunderstood things," replied Kutadanta slowly, "and although I find it hard to endure the light, the truth now dawns on me that there is no separate and enduring self. I will take my refuge in your teaching and find that which is continuing and everlasting in the truth."

Majjhima Nikaya

What, monks, is the world? The eye and shapes, the ear and sounds, the nose and smells, the tongue and tastes, the body and tactile objects, the mind and mental objects—these form the world as we know it.

When an eye and a shape are there, then the consciousness of seeing arises. From this consciousness comes sensation; that which is sensed is thought

over; that which is thought over is projected out-
ward as the external world.

So I declare that in this six-foot-long body with its
perceptions and thinking lies the world, the beginning of the world, the ending of the world, and the
way to the ending of the world.

Majjhima Nikaya

Ananda, the doors and windows of this hall are wide
open and face east. There is light when the sun rises
in the sky and there is darkness at midnight when the
moon wanes or is hidden by fog or cloud. Your seeing
is unimpeded through open doors or windows but
obstructed when there are walls or houses. Ananda,
see now how I return each of these changing states to
its cause and origin. What are these original causes?
Of the changing conditions, light can be returned to
the sun. Why? Because there is no light without the
sun, and since light comes from the sun, it can be returned to its origin. Darkness can be returned to the
waning moon, clearness to open doors and windows,
obstruction to walls and houses, causes to diversity,
emptiness to relative voidness, a confused environ-
ment to unconsciousness, and clear perception to
the awakened state. Nothing in the world goes beyond these conditions. Now when the essence of your

perception confronts these eight states, where can your perception be returned to? If to brightness, you will not see darkness when there is no light. Although these states such as light, darkness, and so on differ from one another, your seeing does not differ, your seeing remains the same.

All states that can be returned to external causes are obviously not you, but that which cannot be returned to anywhere, if it is not you, what is it? Therefore, you should know that your mind is fundamentally wonderful, bright, and pure and that because of your involvement with the things of the world you have covered it up and lost it. In this way you are caught on the endless wheel of becoming this or that, sinking and floating in that sea of endless becoming. Awaken yourself now to your own bright mind.

Surangama Sutra

"When you practice generosity, Subhuti, you should not rely on any object to be the cause of your generosity. You should not rely on words, for they are merely labels. If you practice generosity without relying on causes or labels, you cannot conceive of the happiness. Subhuti, do you think that the space in the east can be measured?"

"No, Honored One."

"Can the space in the west, the north, or the south, or up above or down below be measured?"

"No, Honored One."

"In the same way, Subhuti, if you do not rely on any concept when practicing generosity, the happiness that results is as immeasurable as space."

Diamond Sutra

The clear, calm, stainless, moonlike quality where the shackles which bind the person to becoming this and that, one thing after another, are dropped and allowed to go—this is what I call wisdom.

The one who has gone beyond the rough and dangerous cycle of delusion and repetition, who has left it behind, the one who is contemplative, ungrasping, and doubt-free—this one I call wise.

Sutta Nipata

Subhuti asked: "Is it possible to find perfect wisdom through reflection or listening to statements or through signs or attributes, so that one can say 'This is it' or 'Here it is'?"

The Buddha answered: "No, Subhuti. Perfect wisdom can't be learned or distinguished or thought about or found through the senses. This is because nothing in this world can be finally explained, it can only be experienced, and thus all things are just as they are. Perfect wisdom can never be experienced apart from all things. To see the Suchness of things, which is their empty calm being, is to see them just as they are. It is in this way that perfect wisdom and the material world are not two, they are not divided. As a result of Suchness, of calm and empty being, perfect wisdom cannot be known about intellectually. Nor can the things of the world, for they are understood only through names and ideas. Where there is no learning or finding out, no concepts or conventional words, it is in that place one can say there is perfect wisdom."

Ashtasahasrika

When a person has lived properly and acted generously, he grasps the way things are. He is not dependent on attachments; he is free from anger and aversions; what he does becomes perfect action.

The pureness of perfectly balanced action based on seeing the way things are—this is freedom and the ending of ignorance.

Sutta Nipata

SELF AND SOCIETY

Don't be afraid of doing good. It's another name for happiness, for all that is dear and delightful—this phrase "doing good."

> Whoever would live well,
> Long lasting, bringing bliss—
> Let him be generous, be calm,
> And cultivate the doing of good.
>
> By practicing these three,
> These three bliss-bringing things,
> The wise one lives without regret
> His world infused with happiness.
>
> *Itivuttaka Sutta*

You should be an island to yourself, a refuge to yourself, not dependent on any other but taking refuge in the truth and none other than the truth. And how do you become an island and a refuge to yourself?

In this way. You see and contemplate your body as composed of all the forces of the universe. Ardently and mindfully you steer your body-self by restraining your discontent with the world about you. In the same way, observe and contemplate your feelings and use that same ardent restraint and self-possession against enslavement by greed or desire. By seeing attachment to your body and feelings as blocking the truth, you dwell in self-possession and ardent liberation from those ties.

This is how you live as an island to yourself and a refuge to yourself. Whoever dwells in this contemplation, islanded by the truth and taking refuge in the truth—that one will come out of the darkness and into the light.

Digha Nikaya

Real peace will arise spontaneously
When your mind becomes free
Of attachments,
When you know that the objects of the world
Can never give you what you really want.

Theragatha

People should be able to live without enduring poverty. Grain and other necessities should be given to farmers. Capital should be provided for traders, and proper wages should be paid to the employed. When people have security and can earn an adequate income, they will be contented, without fear and worry. Because of this, the country will be at peace and there will be no crime.

Digha Nikaya

If the bull goes straight when the herd is crossing the road, they will all go straight, because he leads the way. The same among people. If the one who's thought to be highest lives in goodness, the others do so too. The whole realm lives happily if the ruler lives rightly.

Anguttara Nikaya

The Buddha said to Ananda: "Truly, Ananda, it's not easy to teach the way of freedom to others. In teaching freedom to others, the best way is to first establish five things and then teach. What are the five? When you teach others, you must think:

'I will teach in a gradual and sensitive way.
I will speak with the goal in mind.

I will speak with gentleness.
I will not speak in order to gain anything.
I will not speak with a view to harming anyone.'

"If you establish these five things, your teaching will be well received."

Anguttara Nikaya

The one who thinks himself equal or inferior or superior to others is, by that very reason, involved in argument. But such thoughts as equal, inferior, and superior are not there in the one who is not moved by such measurements.

Why should a wise person argue with another, saying: "This is a truth" and "This is a lie"? If such a one never entertains a thought about equal, inferior, or superior, with whom is he going to argue?

The sage who has freed himself from dependence on others and from dependence on words and is no longer attached to knowledge does not risk the smothering of truth by engaging in disputes with people.

Sutta Nipata

Wealth is neither good nor bad, just as life itself is neither good nor bad. All depends on what is done with the wealth. If it is obtained unlawfully and spent selfishly, it will not bring happiness.

But if wealth comes through lawful means without harming others, then one can be cheerful about it. One should remember the dangers of attachment to it and share it with others to create good purposes. If one can keep in one's mind that it's not the wealth, nor even the good purposes, but liberation from craving and wanting that is the goal, then the wealth will bring happiness. One should hold the wealth not just for oneself but for all beings.

Anguttara Nikaya

Living in forests far away from other people is not true seclusion. True seclusion is to be free from the power of likes and dislikes. It is also to be free from the mental attitude that one must be special because one is treading the path. Those who remove themselves to far forests often feel superior to others. They think that because they are solitary they are being guided in a special way and that those who live an ordinary life can never have that experience. But that is conceit and is no help to others. The true recluse is one who is available to others, helping them with affectionate speech and personal example.

Prajnaparamita

Subhuti asked: "How does a person practice all the perfections?"

The Buddha replied: "By not perceiving any duality. Through understanding this nonduality he teaches reality to all beings. With physical energy, he travels widely to teach. With mental energy, he guards against the arising of such ideas as 'permanence or impermanence,' 'good or evil,' and so on. With the perfection of wisdom, he does not consider anything ultimately real but serves all beings with loving attention so that energy, patience, and meditation will be aroused in them. But even though he attends to the minutest detail of whatever must be done, he never grasps it or tries to make ultimate sense of it, because he knows it has no enduring substance of its own."

Prajnaparamita

The Buddha was invited by a brahman to have a meal in his house. But when he arrived, the brahman greeted him strangely, with a torrent of abuse.

Politely, the Buddha asked, "Do visitors come to your home, good brahman?"

"Yes."

"What preparations do you make for them?"

"We get ready a great feast."

"What happens if they don't arrive?"

"Then we gladly eat it ourselves."

"Well, brahman, you've invited me for a meal and you've entertained me with hard words. I want nothing from your preparation. So please take it back and eat it yourselves."

"Never retaliate in kind," the Buddha told his followers. "Hatred does not come to an end through hatred but can only cease through generosity."

Jataka Tale

Abandon wrongdoing. It can be done. If there were no likelihood, I would not ask you to do it. But since it is possible and since it brings about blessing and happiness, I do ask of you: abandon wrongdoing.

Cultivate doing good. It can be done. If it brought deprivation and sorrow, I would not ask you to do it. But since it brings blessing and happiness, I do ask of you: cultivate doing good.

Anguttara Nikaya

A brahman asked the Buddha: "Since nirvana exists and the way there also exists, and since you exist as an adviser, why is it that some of your followers reach nirvana but some do not?"

"Let me ask you something, brahman. Do you know the way that leads to the town of Rajgir?"

"Yes, certainly."

"Now suppose a man came to you and asked you the way there. You might tell him: 'This road goes to Rajgir, so go along it for a while. After a time you will see a village and then a market town but just continue onward. After some more miles you will see Rajgir with its delightful parks and forests and ponds.' But although this man has been carefully instructed by you, he might still take a wrong road westward, while another man, hearing the same instructions, follows them easily and reaches Rajgir. Now, since Rajgir exists and the way to Rajgir exists, and since you exist as adviser, why do you think one took the wrong road and the other the right one?"

"There would have been nothing I could do in this matter, Buddha. I am merely a shower of the way."

"Exactly so. Although nirvana does exist and the way to it exists and I, an adviser, also exist, some of my followers will attain the unchanging goal but others will not. There is nothing I can do in this matter. All I can be is a shower of the way."

Middle-Length Sayings

There are some who wish to perfect themselves and who train themselves in this way: "One single self we shall tame, one single self we shall pacify, one single self we shall lead to final nirvana." But those with compassion should not train themselves in such a way. On the contrary, they should say this: "My own self I will place into Suchness, and so that all the world may be helped, I will place all beings into Suchness, and I will lead to nirvana the whole immeasurable world of beings."

All those of compassion should encourage their minds to think: "Every living being, whether born from the womb or born in any other way, whether they have perception or none, we should bring toward the boundless freedom of liberation. And when this vast and immeasurable number of beings has been liberated, we must not believe that any being has been liberated!" Why is this? It is because no compassionate person who is truly compassionate holds to the idea of a self, a being, or a separate individual.

Diamond Sutra

Just as a cow with a young calf keeps an eye on it even when it is eating the grass, so it's proper for a person to keep an eye on all that can be done for others who are following the path.

Majjhima Nikaya

The Buddha said to the monks:

"People know you as monks. If they ask you, 'Monks! What are monks?' admit that you are monks but say to yourselves, 'We will practice those things which make a monk. In this way being a monk will become a real action, our purposes properly carried out. And our use of the things we need to live on will become fruitful and creative, and when we leave the world it will not be sterile but fertile and full of result.' It is the same for all those who are not monks. However, this is addressed to you.

"What are those things you should practice? Train yourselves to be conscientious and tactful, caring for others. You may think, 'We've already done that. Enough is enough and it has already been done. We've accomplished all we need to do as monks. There's nothing further to be done.'

"But I say and I protest—don't stop your quest while *anything* further remains to be discovered or done. What further needs to be done? You must train yourselves, saying: 'We will become unsullied in our conduct, brilliant and pure. We will neither exalt ourselves nor look down on anyone else.'"

Digha Nikaya

An only son, much loved by his parents, was careless and rude and learned nothing. His parents hoped he would at least look after the land, but he was lazy and dirty and gave them much grief. The neighbors despised him, and his parents finally came close to hating him. This at last touched his heart and he took to religious exercises and prayers but found little help. Hearing about the Buddha, he went to see him and asked to become his follower.

The Buddha told him: "If you would like to be with me and to find comfort that way, the first thing for you to learn is the right behavior. Go back to your home and learn to do as your parents want, continue to recite your prayers, and work hard in your daily life. At the same time, clean yourself up, put on proper clothes, and don't neglect yourself again. When you've learned this, come back to me and you may be allowed to become one of my followers."

Dhammapada

Two kingdoms were on the verge of war over the ownership of a certain embankment.

When the Buddha saw the kings and the armies ready to fight, he asked them to tell him what the cause of this quarrel was. Having heard both sides, he said:

"The embankment has value for some people who live on it from both kingdoms. But does it have any intrinsic value apart from that?"

"It has no intrinsic value whatever."

The Buddha continued: "When you go to battle, is it not so that many of your men will be slain and that you yourselves are likely to lose your lives?"

"Yes, many will be slain and our own lives will be in danger."

"Has the blood of men less intrinsic value than a mound of earth?"

"No," both kings said. "The lives of men and above all the lives of kings are priceless."

The Buddha concluded, "Are you going to stake that which is priceless against that which has no intrinsic value at all?"

The anger of the two kings ended and they came to a peaceful agreement.

Digha Nikaya

Do not live thoughtlessly, in distraction and with deluded aims, outside the universal Law.

Rouse yourself and follow the enlightened way through the world with energy and joy.

Follow the path of enlightenment with happiness through this world and beyond.

See this world as a bubble, a mirage. Be nonattached and death cannot touch you.

Look at this glittering world, it is like a royal carriage. The foolish are taken up by it, but the wise do not cling to it.

The moon comes out from behind the clouds and brightens up the world. So too the one who overcomes his ignorance shines forth.

Better than all the happiness on earth or in heaven, greater than dominion over all the worlds, is the joy of the first step on the noble path.

Dhammapada

The Buddha was staying in the house of Migara. One evening he was sitting on the porch when the Rajah Pasenadi came to visit him and sat down beside him. A procession of holy men passed by, some with long hair, some naked, some with long nails. When the rajah saw them, he rose from his seat, put his robe over one shoulder, and dropped to one knee before them, raising his palms and announcing his name, Rajah Pasenadi. After they had gone, he asked the Buddha:

"Do you think any of those are awakened or have reached the path to awakening?"

"This thing is impossible to know, Rajah. For it's by dealing with someone for a long time that you come to know the virtue, it's by association that you come to know the integrity, it's in times of trouble that you know the fortitude, and it's by deep talking that you know the wisdom."

"It is wonderful that you gave that answer," commented the rajah, "for these people are really informers of mine. They range about, dressed as holy men, and investigate a district for me before I act as judge. When they have washed and dressed themselves in white, they will be ready for all the sensual pleasures."

The Buddha reproved him, saying:

> You should make your observations yourself,
> You should not be the man of someone else,
> Not in dependence on another should you live,
> Nor go about making a trade out of holiness.
>
> *Udana Sutta*

When the Buddha was staying in Savatthi, a rich merchant gave alms for three days, in keeping with his wealth. A well-endowed widow also gave a large amount, and the news of these two almsgivings spread all over India. Then people everywhere started asking, "Does the merit earned by almsgiving depend on large amounts or is it rather in accordance with one's means?"

When the monks heard these questions, they asked the Buddha to settle the matter. He said:

"It is not by the amount that giving is productive of reward but rather by the generous impulse behind it. Therefore even so little as a handful of rice flour given with a pure heart becomes something that will bring great reward."

This statement was repeated throughout India. People gave alms according to their means to beggars and tramps and wandering monks. They provided drinking water in their courtyards and put seats beside the gateways. A wave of generosity spread through the country.

Vimana Vatthu

When the Buddha was dying, he said to his followers: "Just as the earth has hills and grass, healing herbs and nourishing grains for all beings to use, the truth that I have taught is also so. It produces the flavor of wonder and is the healing medicine for the ailments of humankind. I have brought you to abide peacefully in this great treasure. But if you have any doubts, you must ask about them now. Whatever your doubts are, I will try to answer them."

"Honored One, we understand the ideas of no self, of no permanent state, and of the suffering caused to the person by the belief that he has a self and is permanent. He is like one who is drunk and sees the hills and rivers, moon and stars wheeling dizzily about him. Such a one will never understand selflessness and will wander on endlessly in a miserable state. It is because of such an undesirable state that we cultivate the idea of no self."

Then the Buddha was roused from the calm of coming death and said, "Listen closely! You have used the metaphor of a drunken person but you know only the words and not the meaning! The drunk believes the world is spinning when it is not. You still think the self is a something if you believe you should be selfless in order to save yourselves. You believe you should see the eternal as impermanent, the pure as impure, happiness as suffering. But these are concepts and you have not penetrated the meaning. The meaning is that the real self is truth. The eternal is existence. Happiness is nirvana, and the pure is things as they are.

"You should not practice ideas of impermanence, suffering, impurity, and selflessness as though they are real objects like stones or rocks but look instead for the meaning. You should use expedient means in every place and cultivate the ideas of permanence, happiness, and purity for the sake of all beings. If you do this, you will be like one who sees a gem in the muddied water among the stones and rocks and waits for the water to settle before he skillfully plucks it out. It is the same with cultivating the idea of the self as with permanence, happiness, and purity."

The monks were taken aback. They said, "Honored One, according to all you have taught and spoken, we have been asked to cultivate selflessness, leading to the dropping of the idea of a self. But now you tell us we should cultivate the idea of a self—what is the meaning of this?"

"Good," replied the Buddha. "You are now asking about meaning. You should know that, like a doctor, you should find the right medicine for an illness. It is as a doctor that I observed the ailments of the world. I saw that ordinary people believe they have a self and that whoever they meet has a self. They think of the self as within the body. But it is not like that. Because it is not like that, I have shown the fallacy of all the ideas of self and shown that the self is not there in the way it is thought to be. In everything I have said I have shown that the self is not as people think of it, for this is expedient means, the right medicine.

"But that does not mean that there is no self. What is the self? If something is true, is real, is constant, is a foundation of a nature that is unchanging, this can be called the self. For the sake of sentient beings, in all the truths I have taught, there is such a self. This, monks, is for you to cultivate."

Mahaparinirvana Sutra